Celebrate Your Marriage

365 DAILY READINGS FOR COUPLES

by Jay & Laura Laffoon

Jay and Laura would like to thank the board and staff at Celebrate Ministries, Inc. Without you all we'd never have the chance to minister to marriages.

Grace and Diane for editing and layout you two make us look better than we deserve.

All the couples who come to our Celebrate Your Marriage Conferences and Ultimate Date Nights, you keep us inspired!

Our Lord Jesus Christ without whom we'd probably have killed each other by now. (wink, wink!)

Edited by Grace Laffoon

Layout and Design by Diane's Digital Design
didide.com

Preface

Look up the word "encourage" and you will find "To Inspire, to stimulate and to promote." That is precisely what this book intends to do. We want to inspire, stimulate and promote health in your marriage!

Most marriages don't need counseling but every marriage needs encouragement! Our hope as you and your spouse read these daily thoughts is that they will help you "keep on keeping on" in your marriage.

We've intentionally kept these readings short so you can read them together over that first cup of coffee or before you head to bed. We've left room for you to jot down some thoughts as the reading pertains to your marriage and a place for an action step if so desired.

Encouraging you to Celebrate Your Marriage!

Jay & Laura

January 1

If you aim at nothing you'll most certainly hit it!

Living with a purpose is the best way to actualize God's greatest plan for your life and your marriage. What's the best way to make sure that you and your spouse are taking decisive steps forward together? We believe it is with a family mission statement!

Take the time to distill into a brief statement the passions of you and your spouse, and the successes you'd like to experience in the upcoming year.

Then, any time you are struggling to make a decision as a couple, you can evaluate what options line up with your mission statement--best of all, next year, you can sit down to write a new statement and see how far you've come!

Take some time to start your mission statement for the year today!

Thoughts: _____
_____
_____

Action Step: _____
_____

JANUARY 2

Proverbs 17:22,

> *"A joyful heart is good medicine, but a crushed spirit dries up the bones."*

Some days are tougher than others -- but a joyful heart in all circumstances begets laughter and endorphins! Joy is good for our well being, emotionally mentally, physically, and spiritually! This year, remember to keep joy in the forefront of your mind in the every day--even the Mondays.

Thoughts: _____
_____
_____
_____

Action Step: _____
_____

January 3

Our friends Bill and Pam Farrel, authors of Men Are Like Waffles and Women Are Like Spaghetti, encourage couples to find a word for each year--a word for themselves as an individual, and a word for the two of them as a couple!

If you had to choose a word to assign as your purpose for this year, what would it be? What word encourages you and your spouse?

Attach it to your fridge with a mirror, write it on your bathroom mirror, or save it as your phone's wallpaper!

Thoughts: _____
_____
_____

Action Step: _____
_____

January 4

"I don't care."

As a husband I've heard that phrase hundreds of times when I ask Laura where she'd like to go for dinner.

"How about Italian?" "Nah, not in the mood." "Chinese?" "I'm hungry like an hour later." "Seafood?" "We had that last time…" "So where do you want to go?" "I don't care."

When it comes to restaurants "I don't care" really isn't a big deal. What scares us to death are the number of couples who seem to say "I don't care" about their marriage. It's like they've put their marriage on auto pilot and are just coasting along. Live this year with intention when it comes to your marriage. Intentionally communicate on a daily basis. Intentionally date each other-- quality marriages "court" each other throughout life.

And finally, intentionally celebrate the love God has given you for your spouse. This year take the "I don't care" right out of your marriage.

Thoughts: _____
_____
_____
_____

Action Step: _____
_____

January 5

What do you think of when you hear that word "fun?"

A shopping day for Laura, and creative time for Jay--golfing for us both, but not cleaning the house!

Fun in our marriages is something every couple should strive for. Now I can hear some of you right now--but Jay and Laura, we are not fun people--we're actually pretty boring! You don't have to think of yourself as fun in order to create fun.

Fun is being in each other's company and enjoying it! Fun is anticipating your next date together, taking up a hobby together, watching a silly sitcom and laughing together!

Fun means different things to different people.

This year strive to have FUN in your marriage!

Thoughts: _____
_____
_____

Action Step: _____
_____

January 6

Get away and get ahead!

Most couples do not understand the importance of getting away together. Laura and I recommend at least two times a year couples make a plan to get away and get ahead. Once a year get away to "play" together and once a year to "work" (like at a marriage conference) together.

We're aware of all the excuses: it's too expensive, what do we do with the kids, we like to do different things. These excuses are obstacles easily overcome when you understand the enormous benefits that getting away and getting ahead bring to your relationship.

The first benefit is *rest* - our minds and bodies were designed to need rest. The second is *recreation* - refreshing your relationship. Thirdly, *rejuvenation* - this mean to make young again, renewing your love. Finally, *reconnection* - remembering why you fell in love in the first place.

Throughout the next four days, we will be delving deeper into the benefits of getting away and getting ahead!

Thoughts: _____
_____
_____
_____

Action Step: _____
_____

January 7

When Jay was a young boy, his father would sit on the floor outside his bedroom door after Sunday lunch and make him close his eyes until he fell asleep. He was a hyper kid and did not like to rest. His dad, however knew the rest of the family needed a break from him!

There are always benefits to rest--to getting away and getting ahead. When couples get away they enjoy rest.

You may be on an action packed fun filled week away, but you're still getting a "rest" from life and the routine back home. We've been on many vacations that left us exhausted by the end of the week!

But we still found rest. We let our work minds rest, our troubles and trials rest...when you get away and get ahead your find rest for your soul.

Thoughts: _____
_____
_____

Action Step: _____
_____

January 8

Recreation is refreshing to your relationship.

Sometimes we get away for the day. Last week, we were running an errand and planned to be back home within an hour. Instead, we decided to make a day of it and ended up having lunch out and doing some aimless shopping! We were just spontaneous.

Other times we plan a getaway that is for a week. Depending on where we go, we might sit on a beach a read for the entire week, or we might visit museums or historical sites.

All of this is recreation and is good for our marriage. Whether for a day, a weekend, or an entire week, we've all experience the benefit of re-creating.

What getaways can you put on the calendar today in order to refresh your relationship?

Recreate to re-create and refresh your marriage!

Thoughts: _____
_____
_____
_____

Action Step: _____
_____

January 9

Get away and get ahead to rejuvenate your marriage! The definition of rejuvenation is: to make young again; restore to youthful vigor...who doesn't want that?

Now think of that definition as it pertains to your marriage. When you get away and get ahead, you make your love young again you restore youthful vigor to your marriage. And again I ask, who doesn't want that?

We all remember how we felt when we were young and in love. Science tells us that those feeling fade after about 18 months unless we purposefully act to keep the spark alive.

Getting away, if even for a day, to someplace romantic will spark in you and your spouse a new and rejuvenated love for each other and will make your marriage thrive.

So get away and watch those nasty wrinkles fade as you and your love are made new again!

Thoughts: _____

_____

_____

Action Step: _____

_____

January 10

Who are you?

Has that phrase ever crossed your mind when you looked at your spouse? Whether you ask it because they just did something unbelievable or you are asking it because it has been days or weeks since you all have seen each other for any amount of time!

The fourth benefit to getting away and getting ahead is reconnection!

Whatever stage of life you are in--newlyweds that are just starting out, young parents with kids, parents of pre-teens and teens, or empty-nesters that are stuck with only each other--life has a way of disconnecting us as a married couple. Kids, jobs, even ministries can pull us in different directions.

We need to find time--a day, an evening, a weekend, or an entire week - to reconnect with our spouse. Disconnect from the daily obligations and reconnect with each other!

Thoughts: _____
_____
_____
_____

Action Step: _____
_____

January 11

What is love?

Our culture defines it an ooey gooey liver quiver. Dictionary.com defines it as a warm attachment to someone.

Jay and I define love as asking this question: What do I do everyday to show my spouse they are my priority?

Now reality is that this not rocket science! Ask yourself now, "what do I do everyday to show my spouse he/she is my priority?"

It could be something as simple as grabbing your spouse a cup of coffee while you're pouring yourself one, or checking in to make sure they take their vitamins.

Obviously not complicated! But hugely important in a marriage--putting your spouse first. It 's a simple concept but it can be very difficult to do at times.

Love isn't a feeling--feelings come and go. Love is making a commitment for better or worse, richer or poorer, in sickness and in health--til death do us part--to make your spouse your priority!

Thoughts: _____
_____
_____

Action Step: _____
_____

January 12

Eve never had to hear about Adam's mom's cooking!

I know it was the garden of Eden and that it was perfect, but think about it...Adam knew Eve was all he would ever need or want and Eve knew the same about Adam.

One of my mom's favorite sayings is, "there's no perfection in this life," and she's right. Furthermore, there's no perfection in marriage either.

What we have to learn is that the spouse God gave us is all we will ever need in our marriage. Satan will try to get you to believe that there is someone "better" out there, but don't be fooled, we're all fallen creatures that have scars and pasts and baggage.

When you grasp the idea that your spouse, given to you by God, is all you ever need, you start looking at that person in an entirely different light. Looking for the good and not the bad; the helpful not the hurtful, and your marriage grows strong.

Thoughts: _____
_____
_____
_____

Action Step: _____
_____

January 13

1 Peter 3:7 reads,

> "Husbands, in the same way be considerate as you live with your wives, and treat them with respect as the weaker vessel and as heirs with you of the gracious gift of life, so that nothing will hinder your prayers."

This is perhaps one of the most controversial passages of Scripture when it comes to marriage, because no woman wants to be considered as a "weaker vessel." However, if we dig deeper into the meaning of the phrase "weaker vessel," it is actually a term the ancients used for fine china. It was called weaker vessel because it was not as clunky as everyday dishes.

So let's read that again: "Husbands, in the same way be considerate as you live with your wives, and treat them with respect as fine china...."

Now there is a great example of how to treat our wives. And the result? Our prayers will not be hindered!

Thoughts: _____
_____
_____

Action Step: _____
_____

January 14

Laura's love language is quality time. I'll never forget early in our marriage, I was playing basketball over my lunch hour at the local community center. My team had just won the first game and we were taking a water break when Laura walked in and asked, "You wanna go out for lunch?"

I was standing there dripping sweat and with a dumbfounded look on my face. I said "no, we just won so I get to play another game." Laura turned and walked away dejected. What I didn't understand at the time was that Laura wasn't interested in lunch as much as she wanted to spend time with ME.

I realized what had happened quickly and stopped her before she got out the door, and called after her, "Wait a minute honey, let me put on my sweats, I'd love to go to lunch!"

So fellas, surprise your bride and take her to lunch...it's all about saying I love you in a way she'll understand!

Thoughts: _____
_____
_____
_____

Action Step: _____
_____

January 15

Dr. Gary Smalley was our guest speaker at Celebrate Your Marriage and he had some great tips for couples when they argue. They are:

> 1. Don't escalate the argument. This seems simple enough, but we all do it. So, next time you start to argue, step back, take a deep breath and count to 10.
>
> 2. Don't withdraw from the argument. Disagreeing actually means you care. Often withdrawing from an argument doesn't make the problem go away.
>
> 3. Don't belittle your spouse. Name calling is a verbal hand grenade for your marriage. Words like, "you're so stubborn," or, "you're such a brat," can never solve an argument.
>
> 4. Don't project on your spouse something they are not. If your husband isn't ready to buy a new couch, don't call him cheap. If your wife wants a new dress, don't call her a diva.

We wrote these down because they helped us, and hopefully they'll help you too!

Thoughts: _____
_____
_____
_____

Action Step: _____
_____

January 16

Over the next few days, we're going to be looking at five different types of intimacy a married couple should experience. Today we're looking at Social Intimacy--staying best friends!

Most couples admit that when they got married they were best of friends. However as time and life circumstances arise we can drift apart. Ultimately we start "doing our own thing" and as a result lose that friendship aspect of our marriage.

So, here's what we'd like you to do: date! That's right, dating is one of the best ways for a husband and wife to stay best friends.

Gotten into a rut in your dating life? Here's an idea: each of you write down on a separate piece of paper five great dates that you would enjoy.

While your spouse might not pick a date you particularly enjoy, it's important to learn how to gain enjoyment from experiencing your best friend having fun.

So, get your five great dates on the calendar today!

Thoughts: _____
_____
_____
_____

Action Step: _____
_____

January 17

We're looking at five different types of intimacy a married couple should experience. Today is mental intimacy.

Seriously, when we were first married, the difference in intelligence between us seemed so massive. It took years for this phrase to become totally understood by us both: It's not how smart you are, it's how you are smart. Mental Intimacy is about discovering the ways in which you and your spouse are both smart, then deferring to that person's strength in the marriage.

For example:

Jay is smart with numbers--Laura is smart with colors and fabric. So Laura picks out the new couch, and I let her know when there's money in the budget.

Remember: It's not how smart you are, it's how you are smart!

Thoughts: _____
_____
_____
_____

Action Step: _____
_____

January 18

A married couple should experience five different types of intimacy--today, we're discussing emotional intimacy.

Laura the steady one in our relationship. She doesn't have very high highs or very low lows, Jay, on the other hand, can be like a 13 year-old girl. Emotional intimacy begins by realizing you will have very different emotions and emotional reactions from your spouse.

It also means reserving enough emotional energy for your spouse when you are finally together. Spending all of your emotional energy at work or on your kids and leaving none for your spouse is like trying to drive a car with no battery.

Emotional energy is the spark that keeps your marriage alive. On a day-to-day basis, we have to conserve our emotional energy reserve so we can keep connected with our spouse on an emotional level.

Thoughts: _____
_____
_____
_____

Action Step: _____
_____

January 19

Heading into the month of love, we're looking at five different types of intimacy a married couple should experience. Today, it's physical intimacy.

Studies show that one of the best things you can do for the health of your little ones is to let them see mommy and daddy in love. That's right, when children see mom and dad kiss in the kitchen or hold hands on the couch, they do better in school, are healthier both physically and emotionally, and feel they are secure!

Funny how so many Christian couples in our culture try to hide from their kids the very thing that will help them the most! God gave us the gift of physical intimacy and those kisses and hugs are a great model for our kids. And the bottom line? It helps mom and dad stay close as well.

So the next time you're leaving for work, let the little kids see daddy give mommy a goodbye kiss.

Thoughts: _____
_____
_____

Action Step: _____
_____

January 20

We're looking at 5 different types of intimacy a married couple should experience, and today, it's spiritual intimacy.

The easiest way to describe Spiritual intimacy is this: when a husband and wife are both seeking to become like Christ. You see, the more one becomes like Christ, the more one realizes what their partner needs in a spouse.

There are many ways to grow in your walk with Christ, here are just a few:

- Start your day with a quiet time--it doesn't have to be long, just start.
- Join a men's or women's group at your church--surround yourself with others who want to grow.
- Pray together--start simple by thanking God for the gift you have been given in each other.

Remember, becoming like Christ is what your spouse needs most from you.

Thoughts: _____
_____
_____

Action Step: _____
_____

January 21

At times, I feel like no one in my home listens to a word I say! Sometimes it's the kids, other times it's my spouse!

Through much trial and error, I did figure out a few ways to make them listen to me.

Ladies, if you feel as if no one hears you, try the following:

- Make sure they are not doing something else. If I want them to hear me, I need to see their eyes!

- Use a voice that isn't whiny or angry. No one hears an unpleasing voice! I don't listen when my kids whine, so why would I expect them to listen to me if I am?

- Choose your words wisely. Calling them by name gets their attention. Not overloading them with too many words will help the matter as well.

Thoughts: _____
_____
_____

Action Step: _____
_____

January 22

We can all get bogged down and lament about our spouse not meeting our expectations.

Men imagine that when they walk in the door after a long day at work, they will be greeted with a kiss and the smell of a delicious dinner, and children will be playing quietly. Women hold to the dream of a husband who notices when she gets her hair cut, sends flowers on a whim, and helps around the house without being asked.

We all come into marriage expecting our spouse to meet our every need, to be what we need in a spouse. That doesn't happen, it isn't reality!

The truth of the matter is that we need to reverse our thinking and instead of lamenting about our unmet expectations, ask ourselves what we need to do to meet our spouse's needs.

What does my spouse need me to be for him/her?

Thoughts: _____
_____
_____
_____

Action Step: _____
_____

January 23

We believe very strongly in marriage mentoring. In fact, we would go as far as to say every couple needs a mentor couple in their life. Unfortunately, most couples do not have a mentor. The way we found our marriage mentors was actually accidental.

About 12 years ago, our good friends Russ and Joneen started coming over once a week for a time we called "therapy." Basically, we eat finger foods and chat. They are 15 years older than us and have served as our marriage mentors ever since.

Here is what we have discovered as benefits for having a mentor couple in your life:

- Realize you are not traveling down a path no one has traveled before! Mentors can help avoid potholes.

- You receive advice from someone who is not family!

- Hope that you can make it! Mentors give you a vision of the future.

Thoughts: _____

_____

_____

Action Step: _____

_____

January 24

We have just celebrated our 32nd wedding anniversary! We don't say that for the congratulations or the "Hey, look at us"! We say it because marriage is something to be celebrated! No matter how long you have been married, celebrate what God has brought together in your marriage!

We have always gotten away for our anniversary. Even when our kids were young, we made it a habit to get away overnight. The kids always knew that it was our anniversary and we were going to celebrate!

One year when our youngest Grace was in high school, we decide not to go away but to stay home and save the money. When Grace realized that it was our anniversary and we weren't going anywhere, she was appalled!

I can distinctly remember her giving us a "talking to" about the fact that we are "marriage people" and we tell others to celebrate their marriage and here we were not! We would like to encourage you to celebrate your marriage!

Everyday but especially on your anniversary!

Your kids are watching!

Thoughts: _____

_____

_____

_____

Action Step: _____

_____

January 25

Giving Courage

There is something only you can give your spouse. Besides the obvious, you are the only spouse available to ENCOURAGE them—Which literally means to "give them courage." Just think, the words you offer have the potential to push your husband or wife over the finish line on any given day, or to climb any mountain that stands in front of him or her.

I witnessed the power of encouragement firsthand when Jay coached our men's church league basketball team. I wasn't great at getting the ball through the rim—but I loved praising team members anytime one of them did something right. By the end of each game, Jay's voice was almost gone! But the hearts of his teammates were healthy and strong.

And your spouse is no different. Each of us longs to get encouragement, the kind of high-five that helps us soar, from the person closest to us. So find out what words uniquely encourage your spouse by asking . . . and start using those words to give them courage today.

Thoughts: _____
_____
_____

Action Step: _____
_____

January 26

If someone asked what matters to you and your family—what would you say?

When it comes to keeping a family on mission, discovering core values together is the first step toward creating a mission statement that will make your life together count.

Trust us, this first step is relatively painless! All you need is a manila envelope or folder and some slips of paper. For the next month, ask family members to write down one core value a day, dropping it into the envelope. Soon, you'll discover the ideas, people, activities, beliefs or things that matter most to all of you.

Like living in a small town, or regularly spending "fun" time together. Maybe you'll be surprised at a new way to minister together.

On a Saturday, dump out your envelope and categorize the results. Soon, you'll pick a central core value, and finally a simple mission statement that will make your days together fruitful and rewarding.

Check out chapter 5 from our book Make Love Everyday for more great ways to put your mission into action.

Thoughts: _____
_____
_____

Action Step: _____
_____

January 27

What's one way to create celebration, direction, and joy in your family? Identify your core value. That unique, beautiful thing that makes the world go round for everyone together.

Yesterday, we encouraged you to write a value each day for a month and slip it in an envelope. Now we'd like to encourage each family member to narrow it down to 8, then 6. It's important to complete the process based on your true feelings and beliefs, not because something sounds impressive.

Next have conversations and prayers that allow you to sift through all of the things your family holds dear until one value rises to the top—

If you're like us, it might take time, but it's worth it. Because you're identifying that one thing you will intentionally build your lives around. When you find your "one thing," celebrate! You're on your way to becoming an on-mission family!

Check out chapter 5 from our book Make Love Everyday for more great ways to find your family's core value and put your guiding mission into action.

Thoughts: _____
_____
_____

Action Step: _____
_____

January 28

I never cared for math formulas. All you need to do is ask my geometry teacher! But when it comes to building a family that's on-mission, we've found a winning formula that can work for anyone.

A Guiding Mission Statement is built like this:

Start simple with the words TO and THROUGH.

Here's our family's example:

> To encourage others to become like Christ through loving relationships, healthy lifestyles, and stimulating experiences.

TO (insert your family's central core value) + THROUGH (insert 3-5 values that support the central one.)

Without a clear mission, most families feel like they're stuck on a treadmill that never stops. But put a mission in place to guide everyone, and you'll find permission to step off the treadmill and say no to those things that don't further your mission. That's a formula everyone can live with!

Check out chapter 5 from our book Make Love Everyday for more great ways to find your family's core value and put your guiding mission into action.

Thoughts: _____

_____

_____

_____

Action Step: _____

_____

January 29

When it comes to your marriage and family—Are you hoping for progress, or perfection?

A wise man named Abraham Lincoln once said: I am a slow walker, but I never walk back.

On your journey to bringing your family on-mission, finding a central core value and a mission statement are important, as we talk about it in our book Making Love Everyday. But just as crucial is finding a way to honor progress—Not perfection.

Building a "Habits of Our House" list gives you and yours the power and freedom to live by guidelines that honor God and each other, on a daily basis. For example, one habit might be "We take good care of everything God has given us." By the time our family was done, we had 25 habits in all.

Place your list of habits on the wall and notice and praise family members who make progress toward positive habits. This "living document" is an amazing tool for building a home that's filled with celebration. After all, nobody's perfect!

Thoughts: _____
_____
_____
_____

Action Step: _____
_____

January 30

When Aretha Franklin sings the song "R-E-S-P-E-C-T" she echoes the cry of many a woman's heart: "All I want is a little respect!" Philippians 2:3 is a verse that offers more than a little respect. It offers a life-giving alternative to the selfishness humans come by naturally.

"Do nothing from selfishness or empty conceit, but with humility of mind regard one another as more important than yourselves."

Husbands that understand this need report stories like these:

- After a particularly difficult day for her, mostly because of the chaos that is parenthood, I told her how proud I was of the mom she is.

- Or, My husband communicates respect when we are in the presence of others and he says things like, "She's really good at that." He thinks that I have more gifts and abilities than I think that I have!

- And, "I do a lot of "big" programs for the children of our church…it means so much when I hear him say that it went well.

Thoughts: _____

_____

_____

_____

Action Step: _____

_____

January 31

Survey says...
When we took a survey asking men and women what they would change about the opposite sex, we reminded them that they had to list an item their spouses actually had the ability to change.

Both sexes overwhelmingly wanted change in the area of communication. The women wanted men to talk more...And the men wanted women to talk less! Women wanted men to talk more about feelings and emotions, while the men said they wanted the women to do less complaining and criticizing.

After much soul-searching, our friend Pete said it this way. "You know the bottom line? Men don't inherently care about the things women care about, and women don't inherently care about the things men care about."

Underneath the survey, lurked the reality that most of us only want to understand our spouse so we can change them. But we haven't committed to understand them—we've committed to care about them. Maybe it's time to worry less about understanding your spouse, and more about genuinely caring about his or her needs.

Thoughts: _____

_____

_____

Action Step: _____

_____

February 1

Change is inevitable. The truth is our marriages are either growing or deteriorating. And there are two words that help us take the temperature of our relationship with our spouse: Are we causing joy—or pain?

You see, every thought, word or action I have or make brings a degree of either joy or pain to Laura. And the same is true about the way I treat Jay—from the smallest gesture to the biggest sacrifice, everything impacts our marriage. Even the habits we've grown accustomed to can be changed to bring more joy to our marriage:

- I've been working on curbing my sarcasm in public to show respect for Jay.
- And I want to think about the tone of voice I'm using with Laura, not just the actual words I'm going to say.

Over the span of 20 years, small changes can make a big impact. So, how about you: is what you are about to think, say or do going to cause your spouse pain? And how could you choose to bring them joy instead?

Thoughts: _____
_____
_____

Action Step: _____
_____

February 2

Hey guys: I'm guessing you would take a bullet for your wife. Most of us would stand in front of a speeding car, jump off a cliff, or stare down the barrel of a gun to insure our beloved's safety. But the truth is, on normal days of the week, most women are longing most to know they are appreciated and cared for.

So Superman, how about taking a bullet for your sweetheart in the following ways?

- Spend 15 minutes a day in face-to-face conversation
- Hold her with no further expectation
- Play with the kids
- Help with daily household chores

These types of "I see you and I love you" actions communicate volumes to the lady who won your heart. These deeds will bring your wife joy and not pain all of her days. Because the truth is most husbands aren't going to have to take that bullet or jump off that cliff, but dying daily to self will win the heart of the woman you love.

Thoughts: _____

_____

_____

_____

Action Step: _____

_____

February 3

We want to talk about the importance of pre-marital counseling.

There are many great pre-marital counseling plans out there. Google it, and you'll find a bunch. We believe that the best pre-marital counseling is done by a pastor or clergy that you both respect and trust. Why? because you are going to be talking about some very important topics! Topics like: money, intimacy, communication, how to disagree respectfully.

Having that third party there while you discuss these important issues keeps you both on track and focused. You will emerge with a clear plan in front of you and will avoid so many "surprises."

Maybe you're already married and never went through pre-marital counseling--well, it's not too late. Sign up for a class at church, read a book together or get away to a weekend retreat! Just because you didn't have pre-marital counseling doesn't mean you can't address those issues today!

Thoughts: _____
_____
_____
_____

Action Step: _____
_____

February 4

Often we hear from couples that they don't go on dates because they don't know what to do! Here, we are going to help you out! Once a week in the month of February, we are going to give you a date night idea.

This is not a date you need to do tonight or even tomorrow, but rather, some ideas for you to file away in your brain so that the next time you and your spouse are looking for something to do on a date you will have it handy.

Date night idea:

If you have kids in the house, put them to bed early, or at least send them to their rooms--better yet, to a friend's house for the night! Rent a redbox movie or find an old classic on Netflix. Pop popcorn, snuggle on the couch, and enjoy a movie night!

Thoughts: _____
_____
_____

Action Step: _____
_____

February 5

Ladies and gentlemen, the Super Bowl is either nearing! (or perhaps it has passed if so use this tip for next year!) Now, if you are fortunate and have a partner who loves football, then you know how much fun you are going to have watching this game. However, if your spouse doesn't like football, then this can be a stressful weekend. So if this is you, here are some tips for surviving the Superbowl!

Tip #1. Go to a Superbowl party. For the spouse that doesn't like the game, he or she can socialize with the other guests who aren't into the game. One hint, make sure you go to a house big enough for a "game watching room" and a "chatting" room.

Tip #2. If Superbowl Sunday is about one spouse, let Superbowl Saturday be about the other. Spend Saturday doing something the non-football lover wants to do so that he or she feels special too!

Whether at home or at a Superbowl Party you'll both enjoy watching the game.

Thoughts: _____
_____
_____
_____

Action Step: _____
_____

February 6

As we travel around the country and talk to married couples, we unfortunately hear these words all too often: "our marriage is stale," "our marriage is boring," "the love is gone from our marriage," "they're not the person I married."

Here is what we know: marriage is not a one-time decision you made on your wedding day. Rather, it is a decision you make everyday; everyday you wake up and have to decide to love your spouse today.

When your feet hit the floor as you roll out of bed, you have to ask yourself, "how can I love my spouse today? What one positive thing can I find in my spouse today?" Dwell on that!

The day you stood and the altar and said "I do," you said "I choose you," to your spouse.

The staleness, the boring, and the loss of love happens because we forget to choose each other again every day.

Choose each other again today….and every day!

Thoughts: _____
_____
_____
_____

Action Step: _____
_____

February 7

I remember, as I was growing up, every book I read and every movie I watched ended with these words: "and they lived happily ever after."

I think these words become instilled in our brains and we believe that our storybook life will end the same way!

Then we get married, we have kids, we work more than we want to, we become way too busy, and those words, "happily ever after," just become fairy tale fluff.

Well, life is not a fairytale, but we can still live happily every day. How?

Live in the moment--don't be afraid to be spontaneous in your marriage! Drop everything and do something unexpected!

Live for the future--have a plan for your marriage that you and your spouse decide together one that include regular dates.

Live for eternity--trusting your life and your marriage to Jesus. I know that we each love Jesus more than we love each other.

Live happily......every day after!

Thoughts: _____
_____
_____
_____

Action Step: _____
_____

February 8

I remember my first girlfriend, I was in 6th grade. We'd write notes to each other and try not to get caught by the teacher. Notes that said "I think you're cute, do you want to be my girlfriend?"

I'll never forget the first "love note" I got from Laura. It was the day after our blind date. It said "I had a wonderful time last night" and I attached it to a jar full of green M&M's (wink wink).

If you haven't figured it out, today is Love Note Day!

We all loved it when we were dating and we received love notes! So why stop? Let's get creative and continue to send love notes to our spouse. Here are some ideas!

Lunch boxes--nothing says I love you like a note attached to their favorite sandwich.

Emails and texts randomly during the day.

Post-it notes on the bathroom mirror.

Make it a habit to make everyday a Love Note Day!

Thoughts: _____
_____
_____
_____

Action Step: _____
_____

February 9

Last week's idea was a cheap date. This idea is not as cheap!

So, if you need to save your pennies for making this date happen, start now! Planning ahead will make everything go smoother! Everyone enjoys a dinner out at a nice restaurant every so often. There is something about getting dressed up and going out to a "fancy"restaurant that just makes you feel like you are young and inlove!

Get a babysitter if needed. Make reservations ahead of time-- there is nothing worse than planning an evening out and having to wait another hour at the restaurant!

Send flowers early in the day with a card that says your can hardly wait for your date; send text messages all day about how excited you are to go on a date with each other! Anticipation creates fun for the evening!

Thoughts: _____
_____
_____

Action Step: _____
_____

February 10

The big day is closing in…what are your plans?

Did you know Americans probably began exchanging handmade valentines in the early 1700s? In the 1840s, Esther A. Howland began selling the first mass-produced valentines in America. Howland, known as the "Mother of the Valentine," made elaborate creations with real lace, ribbons and colorful pictures known as "scrap."

Today, according to the Greeting Card Association, an estimated one billion Valentine's Day cards are sent each year, making Valentine's Day the second largest card-sending holiday of the year behind only Christmas.

Here's a shocker…Women purchase approximately 85 percent of all valentines.

So? What's the point? The point is, the happily married people celebrate Valentine's Day all year round. But, just like Christmas, we take this day and make it special as proclaim our love to each other.

So, whether a handmade card, a night out at a special restaurant, or that sparkly necklace she's been hinting about, do something to celebrate your love!

Thoughts: _____

_____
_____
_____

Action Step: _____

_____

February 11

How was your day?

This is a typical phrase we use as husband and wife, and it is a great question to ask! It keeps us in daily conversation with our spouse.

We call it a Daily Check Up. We go to check ups for dentists, eyes, doctor, etc. These are usually a yearly check up. Could you imagine not checking up with your spouse for an entire year?

Yet due to life's busyness, this is an all too real situation! Now, usually married couples don't go an entire year with our checking up on each other, but many go an entire year or more without checking up on their relationship.

How was your day? How are you doing? How are we doing?

Asking these questions keeps us in daily conversation with our spouse about each other and about our marriage.

Ask your spouse, "how was your day?" Ask it today and everyday!

Thoughts: _____
_____
_____
_____

Action Step: _____
_____

February 12

Proverbs 29:18 says where there is no vision, the people perish. This was not only true in Solomon's day, but so true today as well--and so true for your marriage. If you don't have a vision or a dream for your marriage, it could perish.

We firmly believe that one of the best ways to divorce-proof your marriage is to dream together as a couple. Cast a vision as a couple; look to the future as a couple. Dreaming can be life-giving to your marriage. When you dream together, when you cast a vision for your marriage together, it gets you and your spouse on the same page. It helps create a bond of love and it gives you hope for the future...together!

So, make a coffee date with your spouse for the express purpose of dreaming together. Some of those dreams may never come true, but some will! Then you will look at each other and say… "remember when this was only a dream?" Now it's a reality!

Thoughts: _____
_____
_____

Action Step: _____
_____

February 13

"I need some space," is not a pleasant phrase to hear coming out of our spouse's mouth. More often than not, it is taken the wrong way. However, giving each other space every so often is healthy for your marriage. We know it's the month of love, but this is still important to your relationship.

Several weeks ago, Jay went golfing with some of his friends-- golfing is something we usually do together. His friends are ourl, and normally a group outing isn't a problem. However, on this particular day Laura wasn't feeling it! She had her own personal plans for the day.

We both had a great day! Now understand, we work together, we live together, we sleep together, we are together every moment of everyday! So this was a much needed day of space. You and your spouse may not have as much togetherness as we do! But space is still a good thing to give each other every so often.

Thoughts: _____
_____
_____

Action Step: _____
_____

February 14

It is Valentine's Day and you know what to do!

Just by way of some encouragement, understand that loves is an action not feeling. It is something that you do.

So DO something today to show your spouse you love them!

Thoughts: _____
_____
_____
_____

Action Step: _____
_____

February 15

We have been giving you Date Night Ideas every week so you have some ideas tucked away the next time you and your spouse go out! No more excuses that you have no idea what to do for a date, no more excuses to keep you from going.

This week's idea was found on Pinterest! (Which, by the way, is a great place to find date night ideas next time you're stumped for one.) It's a $5 Date Night. You each get $5. Go to a mall. If you don't have a mall near you, go to a big box store. You have exactly 30 minutes (or whatever specified time you agree on) to find the best bargain! You can only spend $5! This is for the competitive couple.

Afterwards go out for dinner, ice cream, or coffee!

All too often we got bogged down in the same old date night routine! This idea definitely changes things up and creates some fun!

Thoughts: _____
_____
_____

Action Step: _____
_____

February 16

Here's to the health and the wealth of myself!

That silly phrase is my mom's favorite toast. Who doesn't want to live a healthy life?

According to the book, The Case for Marriage, by University of Chicago sociologist, Linda Waite, a good marriage actually has health benefits for both the men and women involved! The most current results show that married people are more likely to live longer, be physically and mentally healthier, be happier, recover from illnesses more quickly and more successfully, and generally avoid more risky behavior.

Hopefully this will serve as some future incentive--strengthen your marriage, strengthen your health!

Thoughts: _____
_____
_____
_____

Action Step: _____
_____

February 17

Jay was speaking at a youth camp many years ago and had dinner with the camp director. I asked him simply, "Paul, pass the pepper?" He only stared at me, so I asked again: "Paul, the pepper?"

I'll never forget what Paul said next: "Jay, you're a great speaker and are great with the kids, but not once this week have I heard you say please or thank you." My heart sank because I knew he was right.

Saying please and thank you is a perfect example of the one of the "little things" we seem to stop doing once we get married. We get comfortable, we get used to each other--and before we know it we've turned into a couple of inconsiderate roommates.

So, tonight when you get home, intentionally say please and thank you to your spouse and see how your interactions change.

Thoughts: _____
_____
_____
_____

Action Step: _____
_____

February 18

I love spending time on Pinterest! I'll admit, it can be a time waster, but it can also be a great place to find resources for your marriage! For example, I pinned this quote the other day:

> "What counts in making a happy marriage is not how compatible you are but rather how you deal with incompatibility." (unknown)

This is a very true and encouraging statement. So often after a few months or years, we may wonder what we were thinking in marrying this person with whom we have nothing in common! Don't stress! Don't focus on what you see as incompatibility. Rather focus on how you can work through it! Find a hobby you can do together, a TV show that you can both enjoy on Netflix.

No two people are going to mesh together perfectly, but as the quote said--it is how we deal with that incompatibility that makes a happy marriage!

Thoughts: _____
_____
_____
_____

Action Step: _____
_____

FEBRUARY 19

There is no perfect marriage. However, there can be some pretty perfect moments.

I don't know if it's our culture or an underlying human trait, but most of us stand at the altar and have no idea how hard this thing called marriage can be. We think, "well, I love this person, everything should work out just perfectly!" Right? Wrong!

We are fallen creatures living in a fallen world, and as a result there is a little thing we keep bumping into, called pain. The pain of hurtful words or deeds, the pain of unmet expectations, the pain of sinful actions.

What we have to remember is that God gave us our spouse so we can walk this journey together; we have a partner to help carry our load and lighten our burdens. And the beautiful part is experiencing those moments when life is just perfect...together. They can be few and far between, but keep your eyes open, and you'll see your perfect moments too!

Thoughts: _____
_____
_____

Action Step: _____
_____

February 20

So, the month of love is coming to a close. We hope our date night ideas have sparked in you and your spouse not only the importance of dating, but also given you some ideas for future dates!

With the end of February comes the beginning of March, and hopefully the hope of Spring! Today's Date Night Idea involves just that: looking forward to a spring date!

Go to the grocery store together and get your favorite picnic foods. When you return home, fix your picnic food together. Spread out a blanket on the floor if you have a fireplace--lighting it would be a nice touch. If you don't have a fireplace, we use a pre-recorded one on Netflix!

An indoor picnic can be a fun, romantic time! Use the picnic time to discuss date night ideas for the spring!

We hope the Date Nights have given you and your spouse some inspiration to create future dates together!

Date Away!

Thoughts: _____
_____
_____
_____

Action Step: _____
_____

February 21

Every journey begins with one step--marriage is a journey that began with: "I do."

When you stood at the altar and said, "I do," you started a journey that lasts a lifetime. Like every journey, marriage will have its ups and downs, times of crisis, and times of joy. Unlike a journey that has a destination in mind, marriage is not about the destination, but about the journey!

It's about how we enjoy the good times together; it's about how we walk the crises and come out the other side. It is in the journey of for better or worse, richer or poorer, in sickness and health, that we find the joy in this marriage journey

So what do you need for your Journey? Firstly, a guide book, God's word; the right gear for the journey, marriage education; and, the right attitude--"we'll be hiking for a while yet, so let's have fun along the way!" Remember, it is all about journeying through life together.

Thoughts: _____
_____
_____
_____

Action Step: _____
_____

February 22

Hey wives: remember the devotion that swelled in your heart the day you married your husband? It's likely that everyone else at your wedding thought, "Now there's a woman in love!" It may have been 5, 10, or 30 years ago. Can you picture it now? If you're like many of us, you felt, "Whatever my man dreams, I'll go there with him."

The truth is, sometimes the years and the daily grind dull our memories.

Since marriage is seldom a grand gesture—but is more like a daily adventure—why not consider appreciating your husband's needs by following him to:

- his favorite sporting event
- to the garage as he engages his hobby
- to the couch to watch his favorite show (the whole show without getting up!)
- or to the bedroom

The truth is most women will never be called to sail the seven seas or scale a mountain, but daily death to self will win us the devotion of the man we love. And these selfless acts will bring your husband joy in ways that just might amaze you.

Thoughts: _____
_____
_____
_____

Action Step: _____
_____

February 23

Jay's mom likes to say that in marriage you will struggle with three things: Money. Sex. And . . . in-laws. The truth is, we all share similar joys and challenges in our marriages. Isn't it good to know you're not alone?

In our years of marriage mentoring, we've found that men often come to us desperate to understand their wives. And many women are longing to recapture the magic they felt while dating. But the bottom line is we're all longing for—intimacy. That spark that starts small and with time becomes a burning flame of love.

If we think of your love as a fire, it's helpful to remember that over the years, how that fire is stoked will determine the depth of your relationship and the joy you experience together.

So rather than going back in time—or looking for a degree in "wifeology," it's helpful to stoke the 5 areas of marital intimacy: social, mental, emotional, physical and spiritual. Tending to your spark over time will keep those marriage fires burning.

Thoughts: _____
_____
_____
_____

Action Step: _____
_____

February 24

We often hear: God is my #1 priority. #2 is my family.

It sounded good to me, too, until I attended a golf camp where a pro was teaching us how to hit a bunker shot. Toward the end of his demonstration, he simply shared,

> "Here are my priorities: First God. #2 is my wife. And third my children."

In that moment, it felt like my brain exploded. And I concluded that most Christians have their priorities messed up.

Mark 10:8 quotes Genesis when it says, "The two will become one flesh." Not…

The two will become one flesh until the kids come along. It's easy to make the mistake of not recognizing your relationship with your spouse as distinct from your relationship with your children. Yes, you heard us. We believe our children must come third. Rather than spend every night of the week carting your kids to activities, consider your priorities.

Because the single best thing you can do for your child outside of having an authentic walk with Christ is to make your marriage a priority.

Thoughts: _____
_____
_____
_____

Action Step: _____
_____

February 25

Has the laughter gone out of your marriage?

One time a man came to us with a memory from his first marriage retreat. When the leader of the retreat asked "Can you name your wife's favorite flower?" the man actually replied, "Pillsbury, isn't it?"

Often, the day we get married we tend to begin our own "self-improvement" program for our spouse. But part of a healthy marriage is to grow in learning to accept those things that will not change.

A sense of humor, the way your spouse drives, or even the way someone parents.

When Laura was a teen, she spent hours babysitting. But Laura liked to let our son cry for 20 minutes rather than picking him up. We fought back and forth, until I realized that after many nights Laura's way trained Torrey not to cry, even when we put him to bed.

Sometimes different than you can actually be good! Celebrate your marriage today by telling your spouse one thing they have brought to your marriage that has changed your life for the better.

Thoughts: _____
_____
_____
_____

Action Step: _____
_____

February 26

It's a bird! It's a plane! It's superwoman! Able to leap tall buildings in a single bound, this super creature believes she must do everything—And then some.

Experts call it "hurried woman syndrome"—but whatever you call it, stress often wallops women pursuing a career, marriage, parenting, and much more. The expectations we put on women can be out of this world, as I experienced when I tried to be all things to all people. Women around the world report the same pressures, and the health issues that come as a result.

It wasn't until we built our family mission statement that we begin to know what things Laura should say "yes" to, and what "good things" she should give a definite "no" to.

When I prioritized my commitments, I became a healthier woman, wife, and mother. The truth is we women are often trying to be everything, and we simply can't. So rethink your priorities and tell them—superwoman has left the building!

Find out more about a family mission statement in our book Make Love Everyday.

Thoughts: _____
_____
_____

Action Step: _____
_____

February 27

Psst…hey ladies! Here are two little phrases you can use today to improve communication with your husband. Use these at the beginning of a conversation—first, when you want your husband know his services are not needed to "fix" your problem.

The truth is when you share a problem with your guy, he's already working on a solution. That's how his brain is wired. Without verbal cues, your husband will have a hard time figuring out if you need a problem solved—or simply a listening ear.

That's where you come in. When the first thing you say is: "I don't need you to fix this—I just need you to listen," you help your hubbie meet your needs, allowing his brain to track with you. These are the times you left him know you just need to blow off some steam.

Then when you genuinely need help, feel free to say: "I really need your help or advice on this issue or problem."

Chances are, that will immediately launch your guy into action.

Thoughts: _____
_____
_____
_____

Action Step: _____
_____

February 28

Marriage is fraught with opportunities for missed communication—

Or simply missing each other! As we travel around the country, I see a common frustration among many wives. They simply can't understand why their husbands automatically want to be intimate after they share a moment of emotional bonding. For some women, it feels like "strings attached."

But for husbands, the natural physical response to a time of bonding and closeness with his wife is the desire for sex. And he may be scratching his head wondering why that wouldn't be your natural desire, too.

For your husband, a time of deep emotional connectedness naturally leads to his desire for physical connectedness. But as women, our emotions are often spent. That's why it's important we use short sentences to tell our guys what we feel and what we need from them.

When you clearly communicate there are times you simply need emotional support, you will likely find your husband willing to be that shoulder you can laugh, or vent, or cry on.

Thoughts: _____
_____
_____
_____

Action Step: _____
_____

March 1

We get so many questions via email, FaceBook, and our TV show, we thought we would take the month of March and answer some of those questions.

One question we received once read like this: "We both feel criticized by the other, sometimes it is real and sometime just perception, and therefore often we are defensive with each other. What advice or thoughts do you have about this?"

Find something positive first thing in the morning--when your feet hit the floor, straight out of bed, think of one positive thing about your spouse

Watch and listen to tone of voice--when you and your spouse are conversing or even disagreeing, pay attention to your tone of voice as well as that of your spouse

Think before you speak--this is a hard one for some of us. because sarcasm is our spiritual gift! I think through the words that are on the tip of my tongue before I speak them.

Perception beyond what is seen--the body language of your spouse is a great indicator of what is reality and what is merely perception.

Thoughts: _____

_____

_____

_____

Action Step: _____

_____

March 2

Today's question is from a Facebook fan.

"My spouse and I make a very good living, yet we have nothing to show for it. We live paycheck to paycheck. We have had numerous bills go unpaid. We cannot seem to get on top of this situation."

We really see two separate issues in your circumstances:

Budgeting. If you make a good living, it's time to make a budget so you can enjoy it. Dave Ramsey's Financial Peace University or Crown Financial Ministries can easily help you make a healthy budget--but, you have to stick to it

Your second issue is stewardship. You say you've had numerous bills go unpaid--we don't mean to be harsh, but that is a spiritual issue you need to be in prayer about, as not paying bills can damage your testimony for Christ.

You will most certainly solve the stewardship problem when you make a budget and stick with it! You and your spouse can climb this mountain, one step at a time!

Thoughts: _____
_____
_____

Action Step: _____
_____

MARCH 3

"My ex-husband and I have a really good relationship. Our issue is parenting in the midst of this divorce. He tends to let them do more than I do. We are both remarried and each have step children as well. What advice do you have about parenting our own kids, as well as step- kids?"

First, we would highly recommend our friend, Ron Deel of smartstepfamilies.com. He is a leading expert in this field of step-families!

To give you a taste of his material, here are a few of his thoughts:

1. Change your thinking to not view your family as a blended one--because when you put everything in a blender, it gets destroyed. Ron prefers to see a step-family unit as put in a crockpot together--in a crockpot, everything takes time to blend all the flavors together.

2. You and your spouse might be in love, but maybe the kids haven't grown into love yet. Give your kids time to settle into the newness and figure this all out.

3. Be careful not to pit your kids against your ex. It doesn't matter how messy your divorce was, that parent is still your child's parent--good or bad, there is always going to be a connection.

Thoughts: _____

_____

_____

_____

Action Step: _____

_____

March 4

"How can we handle the fact that we came from two very different households when it came to parenting, and now we can't seem to get on the same page concerning our kids?"

What a great question--and not as unusual as you might think! In fact, we ourselves had this same issue in our marriage. Jay grew up in a house with a dad who was a minister and in the military--needless to say, a very disciplined household. Laura, on the other hand, grew up in a laid back, southern household where the whole family would just "go with the flow." As a result, we had to take the time to sit down and define what our parenting style would be as a couple.

Here's the conclusion we came to: the punishment needed to fit the crime. No extreme punishment for minor offenses, and no letting it ride for the bigger cases. Most importantly--especially as the kids got older--we disciplined them together. It let them know we were on the same page, and kept us accountable to being united as well!

Thoughts: _____
_____
_____
_____

Action Step: _____
_____

March 5

"My husband compliments me all the time! I know I shouldn't complain about that but sometimes, it doesn't feel sincere...help! I don't want to whine about compliments!"

I heard once that you should give your partner a sincere, genuine compliment at least once a day--but, we want to avoid making it a box to check on your to do list!

First, it's all about taking the time. To give your spouse a genuine compliment, you've got to take the time to actually think about them personally. It requires you being mindful.

Next, it requires looking for the good in them. Too often we get caught up in seeing all of the petty quirks that bother us about our partner. Leaving the cap off the toothpaste, anyone? By looking to share a compliment, we overlook the small things and focus on the important things.

Most importantly, practicing this keeps you from taking your marriage for granted. Take time to remember why you love and admire them--and then tell them! Don't keep those nice thoughts a secret!

Thoughts: _____
_____
_____
_____

Action Step: _____
_____

March 6

"What do women want?"

Why, women want it all!!

In all seriousness--in order to keep your husband from going nuts, we need to take the time to truly answer that question! What is it that we want? I would say, in general, women want a husband that values her opinion, loves her unconditionally, and views her as a partner.

Gentlemen, women are going to change! We will not always remain the woman you married and we need to know that even with physical, emotional, and maybe even mental changes, you still love us.

So when will your wife feel like she has it all? When you: respect her opinion, love her unconditionally, and walk by her side.

Thoughts: _____
_____
_____
_____

Action Step: _____
_____

March 7

"We have several cell phones, tablets, computers in our home--how can we make the most of technology without losing relationship?"

Technology impacts our relationships and communication--we have to understand technology and its impact. Technology is not a bad thing when used wisely.

As a family you need to embrace technology but also set some boundaries.

Embracing technology come with realizing how it can help. It can provide education for kids, bible apps, and additional modes of communication.

But, we also assign boundaries to our devices--we put our phones and tablets down at 9 pm. No phones at the table during dinner.

Technology is here to stay, so use it wisely!

Thoughts: _____
_____
_____
_____

Action Step: _____
_____

March 8

Today's question is one we get a lot:

"My husband is sick, and the stress on our marriage is extraordinary! I am the caregiver and also have to work full time, as well as take care of household duties and children! How does our marriage survive an illness?"

We can empathize, in the smallest way--last winter, Jay contracted pneumonia in the middle of our busiest tour season. Every weekend we traveled performing our Ultimate Date Nights, and during the week we did absolutely nothing other than the most basic of tasks.

So, if you or your spouse are recovering from an illness, look at what can you do to take some time to recuperate. Surround yourself with a support group that can pray for you and give you emotional support, and even help with physical tasks from time to time. Ask your pastor to connect you with someone in the congregation who has the Spiritual gift of "help." You'll get relief and they will exercise their God given gift!

Thoughts: _____
_____
_____
_____

Action Step: _____
_____

March 9

"How do we capture family time?"

What has worked for our family is setting aside dinner time. Now, it was much easier when kids were younger and didn't have as much going on. We tried really hard to limit the kids to one activity outside of school, That didn't always work, but we tried. It is important to look the kids schedules and adult schedules side by side one week at a time- maybe over Sunday lunch, and map out your week. Set a goal realistic for your family--maybe, to have a certain number of dinners together that next week.

It is so important to start this habit early in your children's younger years so it is already a habit when they are older. Our dinner table is where we get info about their day at school, their work, friends, and future plans for the next day or the next year! Again dinner, doesn't have to be some elaborate meal, just chicken nuggets and salad if in a pinch works! The important part is to be together as a family!

Thoughts: _____
_____
_____

Action Step: _____
_____

March 10

"I can get very frustrated with my husband when it comes to stuff around the house. I feel like I have to remind him of stuff that needs done, and then he gets angry and says I treat him like a child!"

Firstly, don't ask your husband to "help out"--make a chore list together and put it somewhere you can both see it, then either complete the items together or decide how to delegate them out.

You are partners in this marriage--each of you has his or her own to-do list. When, as wives, we think we have to ask our husbands to help out, we have made it our job to make sure that to-do list gets completed, and it isn't!

Don't take undo responsibility and treat him as a child--you have made the chore list, agreed on who does what, now relax! It is Jay's job to change light bulbs in our house...believe me the kitchen stays dark longer than any of us would prefer!

A husband's purpose it to be a teammate with you !

Thoughts: _____
_____
_____
_____

Action Step: _____
_____

March 11

"Neither of us had parents that argued, but we argue...a lot! We wonder if this is normal or is our marriage doomed?"

Conflict, arguments, are both inevitable and necessary in a marriage. There are times when your spouse hurts your feelings, times when your spouse does something that makes you angry. Hurt and anger are normal human emotions, and it is perfectly appropriate to communicate about these emotions in order to work through them in a healthy manner.

When it comes to this type of necessary communication, we take the Triple A method:

Admit your feelings have been hurt. Your spouse might not understand right away, but at least you can get it off your chest.

Apologize for the way you are feeling towards your spouse. In every relationship, conflict comes from both sides.

Ask for reconciliation. What steps can you take to reconcile with your spouse and enjoy a healthy relationship again?

Remember, the era in which your parents were married was very different from the one we're in now--just because you didn't see them argue doesn't mean it didn't happen.

Thoughts: _____
_____
_____
_____

Action Step: _____
_____

March 12

"My wife and I have a never ending conflict. She wants to spend money on nice things, and I would rather spend our money on doing things together."

Well, we can say that couples who have experiences together are happier than those you have nice things, based on all gathered data.

We remember 7% of what we hear, 90% of what we see, and 100% of what we do. The time we spend together is imprinted on our minds eye! Things will break and fade out of style, but memories will get us through the tough times.

We went away for our anniversary this year--this particular place is one we have visited several times over the years, and it was fun to think back and remember all we have done there; the places we have eaten and visited over the years.

This trip, we found ourselves in pouring down rain every night after dinner--this will be a memory for years to come!

Experiences will become a part of your marriage.

Thoughts: _____
_____
_____

Action Step: _____
_____

March 13

"My wife and I are recently retired. We want to make the most of this time, but also know that it can be very trying on a marriage."

Since, as a couple, we haven't reached this stage yet, we decided to share some advice from our friends, David and Claudia Arp.

Be flexible: This is a transitional time, so be willing to try new things. Consider marriage in the second half of life an adventure. Develop a sense of humor and don't take yourself so seriously.

Balance times together and times apart: Too much togetherness can be overwhelming, so make sure you have some time just for you. You need some personal space, but you also need to reconnect.

Keep growing forward: Realize that marriage is a journey, not a destination, and you can decide where you want your marriage to go. It takes work, but even in retirement you can learn new skills to help your relationship grow stronger.

Thoughts: _____
_____
_____
_____

Action Step: _____
_____

March 14

If your spouse does something differently from you, it does not mean that it's wrong. When a spouse insists on having their own way, they in essence are saying, "I have to be in control."

Jay grew up with a military dad. There was a right way and a wrong way to do everything. As we had a conversation about this early in our marriage, Laura would always say, "There's not a right way or a wrong way to do anything".

At least, that was her belief until Jay started making the bed in the morning. After two weeks, Laura said, "I really appreciate you making the bed, but you're doing it wrong." What? Apparently there is a "right" way to arrange the 85 pillows she likes on our bed.

Bottom line is, whether you're controlling about the pillows on your bed or controlling about everything else, the correct answer isn't his way or her way...it's our way!

Thoughts: _____
_____
_____

Action Step: _____
_____

March 15

"Do you have any tips for praying better? In this busy life, prayer is often something I push to the back of my life, yet I know we need to pray more."

Years ago, we started keeping prayer journals. We also started a journal of our hopes and thoughts for our kids at significant times in their lives. Someday we will give these to them!

I have heard of families that have "stones of remembrance"--they have stones they write on when a big moment in their lives happens or when they see an answer to prayer. We have a chalkboard in our kitchen that Laura writes memory verses on, and I am also considering getting a chalkboard that stands that I can put where we will all see it every day with prayers on it so we remember to pray as we walk out the door.

Stormie Omartian has several books that we have read over the years that have helped us focus specifically on praying for my husband and kids.

The important thing is to do it!

Thoughts: _____
_____
_____
_____

Action Step: _____
_____

March 16

"What can I do to love my spouse better?"

How many of us take the time to ask this question--let alone look for the answers!

The answer can be found in Gary Chapmans Love Languages. It isn't necessarily about loving your spouse better, but rather loving your spouse in a way they better understand! We all give and receive love differently. For instance, Laura's love language is quality time; Jay's is acts of service. Doing things like exchanging gifts between us misses the mark!

Don't rack your brain trying to love better--instead, ask your spouse what is it that you can do to let them know you understand them.

Thoughts: _____
_____
_____

Action Step: _____
_____

March 17

Ephesians 5:25 says,

> "Husbands, love your wives, just as Christ loved the church and gave himself up for her."

The last part of that verse is tough when you think about it... Christ died for the church.

Most men I know would take a bullet for their wife, would put themselves between their wife and oncoming danger. Most men would be chivalrous.

I think that verse, however, is talking about something more. How do we "give ourselves up" for our wives on a daily basis? It's found in the little ways we "lay down ourselves," or the little ways we sacrifice for her.

It really is the small things like spending time listening to her day when we'd rather be watching sports, or bringing flowers home for no reason when you'd been saving that money for new fishing gear.

Husbands, love your wives, just as Christ loved the church and gave himself up for her...show her in the little ways every day!

Thoughts: _____
_____
_____
_____

Action Step: _____
_____

March 18

"What does it mean to submit? I get so confused when I hear that verse!"

This is the verse:

> "Wives, submit yourselves to your own husbands as you do to the Lord. For the husband is the head of the wife as Christ is the head of the church, his body, of which he is the Savior. Now as the church submits to Christ, so also wives should submit to their husbands in everything."

As a woman in the twenty-first century (and a wife) I know this wrangles many of us! But I also know that this verse is pretty clear. I understand it this way: we are husband and wife, partners in this thing called marriage, but the buck has to stop somewhere! This verse says it stops with the husband or actually with Christ.

What we neglect to realize is that, if our husband is loving us as Christ loved the church and giving himself up for us, then this isn't a difficult verse to live out.

Thoughts: _____
_____
_____
_____

Action Step: _____
_____

MARCH 19

"My husband is notorious about phubbing! Do you have any tips for overcoming this?"

Now, we can admit, we read this question a few times and had to google what it actually meant! "Phubbing" is phone-snubbing!

You know the feeling when the cell phone is the most important thing! Everytime the phone makes any noise whatsoever and your spouse picks it up immediately...even if you are out on a date!

Jay has all notifications turned on for everything on his phone, so when he gets a Facebook comment or an email comes in, he won't miss it!

Laura has this wonderful app called Find Friends, so she can see where the kids are all the time. It can be a bit obsessive!

We plug our phones into a battery station every night around 9 pm and don't pick them up again until morning.

We agree ahead of time, when going out, we won't check our phones when there is a lull in the conversation!

Thoughts: _____
_____
_____
_____

Action Step: _____
_____

March 20

So many of us feel like we don't measure up. Most of us are grew up with dreams of being an astronaut, or a doctor, or professional athlete, but most of those dreams didn't materialize.

Many marriages are stuck in downward cycles because one spouse or the other (or both) are carrying around wounds of deep-seated failure from past and our present failures.

Your spouse married you--all of you! No one is perfect; your failures, past and present, are part of what makes you who you are. Learn to trust and communicate to your spouse when you feel like you've failed. Your biggest fan will still love you and will help you as you strive to overcome those failures and become all God created you to be!

Thoughts: _____
_____
_____

Action Step: _____
_____

March 21

"I wish my husband could read my mind and just know what I need him to do! I feel like a nag when I constantly have to tell him to do something!"

Ladies, we need to be specific with our husbands. One busy mom said that she used to feel overwhelmed with household chores, wishing her spouse would help her. She now realizes that the only way he knows her needs is when she tells him. "Most often," she says, "when I simply say, 'Honey, will you tuck the kids in tonight while I get the kitchen cleaned up,' he is glad to help." She's discovered that a few words are all it takes "to change a resentment-filled, stressed-out night into a team-effort bonding time."

The best thing we can do is to change the way we think. We are not nagging, we are not requesting help, we need to simply state a fact. Men understand facts.

Thoughts: _____
_____
_____

Action Step: _____
_____

March 22

"My wife is a worrier! I don't understand it and can't seem to say the right thing!"

"Just don't think about it," is what Jay always says! Women have no idea what that means. If your wife is worried that her best friend suddenly isn't talking to her, she has no way to not think about it. When the kids are out, she is worrying about them, and when they get home, she worries if they had a good time!

Men think about 5 things: work, play, intimacy, food, and nothing. As men, we have the ability to think about only these 5 things and our favorite one is nothing!

Women think about everything! When something bothers us, we dwell on it--we can't fathom thinking about nothing!

Realizing these differences can go a long way in understanding each other and helping each other in those times of great worry!

Thoughts: _____
_____
_____
_____

Action Step: _____
_____

MARCH 23

"My husband is angry a lot of the time. I don't know how to handle it and just wish he could do something to deal with his anger."

Shaunti Feldhaun has the best answer to this question--one I had never thought of before.

"Ladies, if you think crying when feeling unloved is an acceptable response during a relational conflict, would you be surprised to know that anger is often a man's response to feeling disrespected during relational conflict?" Pause and let that sink in.

Before we clobber the guys about the need for Anger Management 101 let's put this in perspective. We feel we deserve the right to cry without being accused of being manipulative or disregarded as an emotional basket case. But when our man expresses anger in his communication during a conflict (in response to feeling disrespected) we often treat him as if he's broken all the "rules of engagement" for relational conflict.

I had to let that sink in and really mull it over! Let's hope I can remember it next time we disagree!

Thoughts: _____
_____
_____
_____

Action Step: _____
_____

March 24

"I was talking to a woman the other day who was complaining that her husband tells the same stories over and over and it drives her crazy! She also commented that he talks way too much!"

Apparently you have a unique husband! Most women complain that their husband doesn't talk enough! Listening is what you signed up for!

We may not always be interested in what our spouse is saying, but one thing we live by is, "if it is important to them, it is important to me!" It is why Laura learned to play golf, and it is why Jay listen always entertains the next decorating idea for the house.

Listening is more than just hearing the words your spouse is saying--be thankful for a spouse who communicates!

Thoughts: _____
_____
_____

Action Step: _____
_____

March 25

"How do we get back on track?"

Remember when you were newly married? Life seemed so easy then! After work, you would enjoy each other's company over a thoughtfully prepared dinner, spend countless hours of sharing about your day. How long did that last? Life gets busy and can throw us off track in our marriage.

Work, children, committees, church, bills...we are just too exhausted with life to get our marriage back on track!

Here are a few tips on how to put your marriage back on the right track:

- Make your marriage the only priority--even if just for a few minutes a day.
- Make a list of outside activities and the priority they hold--you may have to cut some.
- Make a date night calendar--it may be only once a month, but the time spent together without the kids will reap great dividends.

Your marriage may be off the tracks a bit, but with a little prioritizing and effort you can right the train!

Thoughts: _____
_____
_____
_____

Action Step: _____
_____

March 26

One of my love languages is gifts. I love getting surprised with a gift for no reason at all--gifts say, "I was thinking about you!"

Now, I hear some of you now--gifts cost money, and I can't spend money all the time! Here's the deal; gifts don't have to cost money, just time and thought. Actually, the simple, small gifts mean more. A fresh picked flower from a field, a note in a lunch bag, an afternoon text, a foot rub after a long day.

Too often we think gifts are something we need to go out and buy, when really a gift is an unexpected thoughtful act of love!

We need to build into our marriage the act of looking for the small things we can "give" our spouse that doesn't cost but is priceless! This will build gratefulness and appreciation into your marriage!

Thoughts: _____
_____
_____

Action Step: _____
_____

March 27

What happens when you put food into a blender?

It purees all together very quickly....

What happens when you put food into a slow cooker?

It cooks a long time and blends well together.

This is what our friend Rod Deal, of successful stepfamilies.com, says stepfamilies should work towards--being a slow cooker instead a blender. Slow cookers allow for time to do the job, versus just putting everything together in a blender and pushing puree.

Parents who are in a remarriage with children need to realize that "blending" is not going to happen quickly. There are way too many variables to allow this to happen. Rather, look at your new family as a slow cooker: you want to take "blending" slowly to allow each family member the space they need to adjust.

Step-families need to realize that all family members are going to add to the flavor to the family in their own time.

Thoughts: _____
_____
_____
_____

Action Step: _____
_____

MARCH 28

Different stages of life bring new challenges to a marriage.

We tend to hear mostly from the couples that are in the raising children stage of life. The other day, we received an email from a woman in hot-flash-stage of life!

Laura could identify with her all too easily! When we first moved to Michigan, Laura was freezing all the time. She was always putting on 2 layers--a t-shirt under that sweatshirt, leggings under those sweatpants. It worked! Looking like a sumo wrestler was a good compromise for being warm.

Now? Laura's burning up all the time! It happens....We can't even sit next to each other in our favorite chair because it causes to much heat! So now we hold hands from a distance!

Getting old happens, we laugh and keep growing together!

Thoughts: _____
_____
_____

Action Step: _____
_____

MARCH 29

What would your day be like if you didn't check your Facebook page, read your twitter feed, add a picture to your instagram, look up a DIY project on youtube, make a board on Pinterest, or check your email? We would probably have a few more free hours in my day!

Now ask that same question about your marriage...what would your marriage be like if you took those activities, unplugged for a day, and instead spent time with your spouse? Technology is a good thing but, unfortunately, we need to have some rules in order to use it wisely!

We have a few rules when it comes to tablets, phones, and other devices in our house:

- None are allowed at the dinner table.
- When I am talking to you, do not check your phone.
- None are allowed in bed.

Take the challenge and unplug for a day. Let us know the results!

Thoughts: _____
_____
_____
_____

Action Step: _____
_____

March 30

"How do you two do it?"

We work together, we eat together, we exercise together, we grocery shop together, we sleep together, we watch tv together... that is a lot of togetherness!

We get asked all the time, "how do you do it?" Many times, the person asking wants more togetherness with their spouse, and others not so much!

A few issues can come as a result of all this togetherness:

Working too much: we can spend too much time in our office and not enough time in our home. We also have a tendency to talk about work when we are on a date.

Serious focus time is needed to get out of the office and get on a date!

Taking each other for granted: because we are together 24/7, we tend to not always see each others emotional needs.

Time apart is the answer! Laura goes shopping and I go golfing! Just a few hours is all that is needed to regroup and recharge.

Thoughts: _____
_____
_____
_____

Action Step: _____
_____

March 31

We asked couples the greatest challenge for their marriage:

"Our greatest challenge currently is working opposite shifts We are in our late 50's, in our second marriage. But we are challenged in that our jobs are complete opposite hours. I work a regular day shift Monday-Friday. My husband works the evening shift, Monday through Thursday. Help!"

Here are a few suggestions for making this work:

- Split up household chores so each spouse has some responsibility when not at work.
- This will keep the weekend free of household duties and free those hours up to enjoy each other's company.
- Enjoy weekend meals together, since you don't have nightly dinners during the week for conversation.
- Text each other during work hours to remind your spouse you are thinking of them!

While this couple's schedule is definitely not ideal, it can be handled with a little bit of effort and planning ahead!

Thoughts: _____
_____
_____
_____

Action Step: _____
_____

April 1

Another greatest challenge question:

"Our greatest challenge is financial debt. We have lots of medical debt due to a health issue I am now addressing. There just isn't enough money on my husband's salary."

We may have said it before, and if we have it is worth repeating! Get help!

Budget, budget, budget!

I used to dislike that word immensely until I came to realize that when we lived by a budget, we actually experienced more financial freedom than without it! Dave Ramsey's Financial Peace has helped countless couples get back on their feet again.

The stress of financial debt, illness, heaped on top of just the daily stress of life can be way more than a couple can handle. Don't be afraid to seek out help at your church or in your community!

In marriage, you will have disagreements about three things: money, intimacy, and family. Seeking help in any or all of these areas when you reach an impasse is always a good idea!

Thoughts: _____
_____
_____
_____

Action Step: _____
_____

April 2

"Our number one challenge at this time is finding time to communicate. Not just to gab, but to sit down and talk about important things, what has gone on during the day, about the kids, ourselves, our jobs. Wish we had more time to do that."

I can hear in this woman's heart a real desire to connect with her husband. Connection in marriage happens in many ways but the one most important for your wife, gentlemen, is to sit and talk about more than just the plan for the day or how work went.

I know for most men this strikes fear in their heart! It doesn't have to! Just sit down with your wife and start by asking about the kids and let her talk. Then ask about her friends, and let her talk….

Find a few good questions to ask, and let her talk!

Oh, and you do have to listen!

Thoughts: _____
_____
_____

Action Step: _____
_____

April 3

"For all have sinned and fallen short of the glory of God."
(Romans 3:23)

We have all messed up, sinned, made mistakes, fallen, sinned. It's human nature; it began with Adam and it continues with us.

"If we confess our sins, He is faithful and just and forgives our sin and cleanses us from unrighteousness." (I John 1:9)

We all understand this if we are believers--the hard part is forgiving ourselves. We can bring that unforgiveness into our marriage. Our pasts can at times keep us from living in the present.

Picture yourself as a traveler bogged down with an unimaginable amount of suitcases. You have them over both shoulders, two in each hand, a few backpacks on your back, even some fanny packs are strapped on! As you are traveling, you run into someone who wants to give you a gift….what do you do? You have to let go of some of your luggage in order to receive the gift.

Your marriage is the gift. Let go!

Thoughts: _____
_____
_____

Action Step: _____
_____

April 4

Answer this question: what do you expect from your spouse?

Creating realistic expectations, and extending grace when expectations are not met is a struggle in most marriages.

In its definition, expectation is something hoped for, not guaranteed. We need to see expectations we have for our spouse as a hope, not a rule.

I expect to have dinner nightly with my family; yet, the reality is that we all have such crazy schedules, we do well to have dinner together three times a week. I expect to have a clean house when I get home from work. Reality is that when the kids have been home sick all day, the house is a disaster! I expect my husband to take out the trash after dinner. Reality is he doesn't even realize it is full!

We all have unmet expectations in our marriage. Giving grace when reality is not what we had hoped for will create an atmosphere you can live with in your home!

Thoughts: _____
_____
_____
_____

Action Step: _____
_____

April 5

I was chatting with a man who was almost in tears as he expressed the fact that, in his home and in his marriage, he felt not needed. This is a real challenge for couples with young children or children who are ill in some way and need a great amount of attention.

Ladies, this one falls on us. I know this, because I am a mother and more times than I would like to admit, I have had the thought, "Oh Jay can take care of himself, the kids need me!"

We have to make sure that we are focusing on our husbands more than our children. There is nothing we can do more for our kids than to love their father. We have seen more marriages fall apart as they enter the empty nest stage, because the focus of their marriage has been on the kids rather than each other.

Your husband doesn't need you like your children do, but he does need you!

Thoughts: _____
_____
_____

Action Step: _____
_____

April 6

"If you can't say something nice, don't say anything at all."

How many of us heard that growing up? How many of us actually live by it--especially when it comes to our spouse?

Disagreements are going to happen in marriage--you are two different people with two different opinions and they will clash from time to time. The struggle is how to clash fairly.

- Listen and repeat back what you hear: "So what I hear you saying is…"

- Ask, "how can I help?" versus, "here is what I think you should do…"

- Never discuss something important in the heat of an argument--in other words, if you are both too angry to be calm, call a time-out.

Arguments are going to happen. Just don't argue dirty.

Thoughts: _____
_____
_____
_____

Action Step: _____
_____

April 7

Jay is a dreamer--Laura loves the details. This used to be very frustrating in our marriage. Anytime Jay would voice a big idea, Laura would get tired just thinking of all the little details that would have to come together to make that happen.

At the same time, whenever Laura would see a fun home renovation project she was interested in, the thought would frustrate Jay! All he could see were the dollar signs--but this was the way Laura dreams.

We as individuals communicate differently, we dream differently, we hear differently....the important thing is to understand those differences.

Thoughts: _____
_____
_____

Action Step: _____
_____

April 8

Our phones are like our own little worlds, the piece of our lifes we think we don't have to share. We, for some reason, are protective of them from others--even from our spouses.

I had a gentleman tell me the other day that what is on his phone is none of his wife's business--I instantly corrected him! You are married, therefore what is yours is hers and vice versa.

By the way, if you have nothing to hide, there shouldn't be a problem!

Your phone is not your own!

Thoughts: _____
_____
_____
_____

Action Step: _____
_____

April 9

Another great question from a Facebook fan:

"My wife and I have our own hobbies/interests. I like to play sports and she scrapbooks and paints. Should we be trying to develop some common hobbies?"

Yes! Having a hobby you enjoy together has benefits:

- You automatically have a built-in date. In the summer, we have golf dates.

- It gives you something to talk about that is not the kids or work. We relive our golf games way too much, and we are also very competitive!

- It meets your need for companionship in your marriage!

Developing a hobby together will strengthen your marriage.

Thoughts: _____
_____
_____

Action Step: _____
_____

April 10

This was an interesting question from a Facebook fan:

"My wife's love language is acts of service, and I speak it very well! I do most everything around the house, the dishes, the laundry, clean….here is my problem, I have teenagers in the house who do nothing, because I do it all in order to love my wife!"

We applaud him for speaking his wife's love language! But let's get to the parenting issue.

Our kids have done their own laundry since they were in junior high. Before that, when they were young, they had to put their own clothes away after the laundry was done.

Kids and teens need to have chores to do around the house. This should have nothing to do with your spouse's love language--it has to do with teaching your children!

Thoughts: _____
_____
_____

Action Step: _____
_____

April 11

As defined by Webster, a cliche is anything that has become trite or commonplace through overuse. Cliches like, "the grass is always greener on the other side of the fence."

The institution of marriage has become a cliche of sorts in our society. More couples are not marrying and cohabiting instead. Our younger generation does not see the need to get married. This should an alarming pattern for the church--not to mention, we have recently seen marriage re-defined in our culture.

We thought we would take a look at cliches in the month of May in order to show that they can still teach us about ourselves, even though we may think they are trite and commonplace! Marriage is not a cliche--it is a beautiful gift from God! Marriage has been around since the beginning of creation and is still valuable today, as are the cliches we are going to use in the next several weeks.

Thoughts: _____
_____
_____

Action Step: _____
_____

April 12

"An ounce of prevention is worth a pound of cure."

Most of us understand that statement when it comes to our health; we try to exercise, eat right, take vitamins and see the doctor once a year. We do all of this because we know it's the right thing to do so we make it a priority!

So why don't we take that same advice and apply it to our marriage? All too often, couples wait until problems become insurmountable before seeking help! Then it takes a lot of hard work and loads of time to dig themselves out of that hole.

What does an ounce of prevention look like for a marriage? Daily communication, so you stay connected; weekly dates to keep the romance alive; and a planned getaway once or twice a year so you can focus on each other. This will all work to keep your marriage healthy.

Remember, an ounce of prevention is worth a pound of cure!

Thoughts: _____
_____
_____

Action Step: _____
_____

April 13

Sometimes, going back to square one means we've made a mistake and have to start all over again. But in marriage, that cliche can take on a whole new meaning!

Back to square one in your married life means remembering why you fell in love with your spouse in the first place; his smile, her laugh, his integrity, her patience. Life is hard, and from time to time we begin to focus on the negative about our spouse.

But Philippians 4:8 reminds us:

> *"Finally, brothers and sisters, whatever is true, whatever is noble, whatever is right, whatever is pure, whatever is lovely, whatever is admirable—if anything is excellent or praiseworthy—think about such things."*

So, when it comes to your spouse think about whatever is true, noble, right, pure, lovely, admirable, excellent or praiseworthy. The next time you're starting to become critical of your spouse, remember this verse and take it back to square one!

Thoughts: _____
_____
_____

Action Step: _____
_____

April 14

"You can't teach an old dog new tricks."

That cliche is really a cop out, because old dogs can learn to do new tricks, and Jay is living proof. Well, not that he's a dog or old but you get the point.

Jay's challenge to men all over the country is to develop a new "positive" habit in their marriage every year or so. This is very important in a marriage, because the extra effort you put into that new habit means a lot to your wife.

The last habit Jay developed was really special in our marriage. Simply put, he started making the bed every morning. He never made the bed for the first 30-odd years of our marriage, then one day he just started…now, mind you, he didn't do it the right way, but it was the thought that counted.

So whether you are an old dog or a young buck, build a new habit into your relationship today!

Thoughts: _____
_____
_____
_____

Action Step: _____
_____

April 15

"Don't get your knickers in a knot."

My mother used to say that to me all the time--and I never wore knickers! As a child I was quite an "over-reactor," so she also often asked me if what was upsetting me would matter in 100 years.

In our marriages isn't it odd how silly some of our disagreements can be? I mean, seriously, think about your last tiff, dust-up, or disagreement. Was it about something that really matters? Or was it over something silly?

There are some things that really matter: your faith in Christ, how you raise your children, how you steward your time and money. Most of the rest of life really won't matter in 100 years.

So the next time you feel your knickers are tying themselves in a knot, ask yourself; is this really going to matter in 100 years?

Thoughts: _____
_____
_____

Action Step: _____
_____

April 16

"Early to bed, early to rise makes a man healthy, wealthy, and wise."

That phrase drives me crazy! But whether you and your spouse are night owls or early birds isn't the point; the point is to go to bed and get up at around the same time.

Now, we understand there are certain jobs that make going to bed at the same time impossible--but if you can, you should, and here's why: first, it puts you and your spouse on a similar schedule; second, there is a connection that occurs when you drift off to sleep together; finally, it sets a great example for your kids.

So, whether you like to stay up late or get up early, do it together and reap the benefits in your relationship.

Thoughts: _____
_____
_____

Action Step: _____
_____

April 17

"Firing on all Cylinders"

This cliche is used to indicate that an engine is running smoothly and powerfully. So here's a question...is your marriage firing on all cylinders? There are four main "cylinders" that a marriage engine needs running smoothly.

First is money. Are you on the same page when it comes to budget and spending? If not, sign up for a class like Dave Ramsey's Financial Peace University.

Second is intimacy. Are you being clear about ways you and your spouse can stay close?

Family is the third cylinder. Have you discussed clear boundaries for your family when it comes to your children and extended family?

And finally, communication. Men and women communicate differently, so this is often the hardest one to get firing--but when this one sputters, it impacts the other three!

Make a coffee date at least once every 3,000 miles and ask your spouse if your marriage if Firing on all Cylinders!

Thoughts: _____
_____
_____
_____

Action Step: _____
_____

April 18

"The grass is always greener on the other side of the fence."

When we moved into our current house, it had not been lived in for over a year, and boy, did the yard show it--and to make matters worse, my neighbor had an immaculate, lush green lawn that he took great care of. I asked him how he kept his lawn looking so good. He replied, "three simple ingredients: water, sunshine and fertilizer."

In marriage we can run into the trap of thinking about greener grass in someone else's yard, and that's very dangerous. So how do we keep the grass green in our marriage? Three simple ingredients:

Faith--in God and His son Jesus.

Hope--in the future God has in store for you and your spouse.

Love--that is unconditional. Remember 1 John 4:19, "we love because he first loved us."

Those three ingredients will certainly keep your marriage growing!

Thoughts: _____

_____

_____

Action Step: _____

_____

April 19

"Haste Makes Waste."

No where is this more true than when making big decisions as a couple. We've always counseled couples to make big decisions as slow as possible. Big decisions like buying a house, a job change, where to send the kids to college--these are big decisions that can have a long term impact.

Here are three suggestions before you make your next big decision:

- Seek the counsel of wise friends. By wise friends we mean older friends--find couples who are further down the road than you are and can give you sound advice from experience
- Make a pro-and-con list. Actually write it out so you can see it on paper. This will help clarify things in your mind
- Bathe it in prayer. Offer your big decisions up to the Lord and ask Him for peace about your decision. That peace will keep you from having second thoughts.

Simple suggestions to keep you from a hasty decision.

Thoughts: _____
_____
_____
_____

Action Step: _____
_____

April 20

"If I've said it once I've said it a thousand times."

One listener writes in: "Why do I have to repeat myself so often? There are some days I have to tell him the same thing several times!"

Here's something we've learned in 31 years of marriage: if Laura has something important to say that she doesn't want to repeat, we follow these simple rules:

Don't say it when he's hungry.

Don't say it when the TV is on.

Don't say it if his phone is in his hand.

When trying to communicate with your husband, it is important to have his undivided attention, so if he's hungry or the TV is on (even in the other room), don't attempt it.

Make sure you have his undivided attention by looking each other in the eyes when communication something important.

Thoughts: _____
_____
_____

Action Step: _____
_____

April 21

"There's a Kodak moment."

We've heard it all too often--social media has us all comparing our lives "B-roll" to everyone else's Kodak moment!

Comparison kills, and yet we do it all the time. Here are some reminders why we should compare our lives or our marriage to anyone else.

God's Thumbprint has been placed on you and your marriage. While we are all similar, God has made your marriage and your children unique, so rest in the knowledge that God created you to be exactly who you are!

God's To-Do list has your name is on one line. Did you know that God created you and your spouse for a specific purpose? That purpose is to glorify Him and to do it in a way no other couple can, using your gifts and your abilities.

God's wallet contains a picture of you. I know God doesn't need a wallet, but you are His child and His love for you is unconditional.

So don't compare--you're a child of the King!

Thoughts: _____
_____
_____
_____

Action Step: _____
_____

April 22

"Life is a bowl of Cherries."

Many of you have never heard the song but the lyrics are a gentle reminder to us all

Life is just a bowl of cherries. Don't take it serious, Life's too mysterious. You work, You save, You worry so. But you can't take your dough when you go, go, go.

So keep repeating "It's the berries." The strongest oak must fall. The sweet things in life to you were just loaned. So how can you lose what you've never owned.

Life is just a bowl of cherries. So live and laugh, aha! Laugh and love. Live and laugh, Laugh and love, Live and laugh at it all!

It almost sounds like a proverb written by Solomon. Life is LIFE with a capital L and everything here is just on loan to us from God so enjoy every minute!

Soak up the sun. Smell the roses. And remember...

Life is just a bowl of cherries

Thoughts: _____

_____

_____

Action Step: _____

_____

April 23

"The more we learn the less we know."

I remember hearing the story about the first-year lawyer who was taken to lunch by his firm's managing partner.

The young lawyer asked "How do I become a successful lawyer?"

The partner responded, "By gaining experience."

"How do I gain experience?"

The partner responded "By making mistakes."

"So in order to be successful, I have to make mistakes?"

Sounds a lot like marriage doesn't it? We have been married 31 years and we've lost count of the number of mistakes we've made.

Here are two principles we try to live by: first, when we fail we get up and try not to make the same mistake again; second, we know that a good marriage is made up of two great forgivers.

These two principles will go a long way into building a successful marriage!

Thoughts: _____
_____
_____
_____

Action Step: _____
_____

April 24

"No strings attached."

Wouldn't it be great if we could live that way--with no strings attached? Unfortunately, in marriage we all tend to play the tit-for-tat game. It's really no way to live life, and certainly no way to build a strong marriage.

Once, Jay brought home a bouquet of flower that said, "To Laura, love Jay--just because." No strings attached. That day changed our marriage forever as we realized how powerful the idea of loving with "no strings attached" was.

We challenge couples to do something for their spouse "Just Because" with no strings attached. Here's a few ideas:

Detail her car

Fix his favorite meal

Buy her flowers or a piece of jewelry

Whatever you do, do it just because--with no strings attached!

Thoughts: _____
_____
_____
_____

Action Step: _____
_____

April 25

"On the tip of my tongue."

I was counseling with a man who was worried he was going to lose his wife and their marriage would be destroyed.

As we talked, I asked him, "When was the last time you paid your wife a genuine compliment?"

He hung his head and said, "I can't remember." He went on to convey that many times a compliment was on the tip of his tongue, but he just didn't get it out.

In our marriage, Jay's love language is words of affirmation--and, unfortunately, Laura speaks fluent sarcasm. Just a few years into our marriage, it hit me: I need to be Jay's biggest fan. I'm his wife for crying out loud, and if I can't tell him good job or that-a-boy then who will?

Take some time today to compliment your spouse. Let them know how much you think of them and then say it in front of your kids or your friends. Build each other up and build your marriage!

Thoughts: _____
_____
_____

Action Step: _____
_____

April 26

Early in our marriage, Laura would often ask, "Penny for your thoughts?"

She just wanted to know what he was thinking at the time because it appeared he was lost in deep thought. Imagine the surprise when he said "nothing."

I said, "How can you be thinking of nothing, that's impossible! You have to be thinking of something."

Ladies, I know this is hard for you to understand because of the way your brain works, but your husband can actually think of nothing. We all have a special place we can go in our brains where it's just blank and stress-free where we don't have to think.

So the next time you ask your hubby, "watcha thinking?" and he says nothing, don't get mad at him, understand this is how God made him.

Thoughts: _____
_____
_____
_____

Action Step: _____
_____

April 27

"Quicker than a New York minute."

We're empty nesters. We've moved into a new realm in our marriage--no kids! Truthfully, it seems like it happened quicker than a New York minute! Today we're going to share some tips for you empty nesters.

First, establish boundaries with your adult children. Let them be adults! I know I struggle with this when it comes to our daughter, Grace. She's lived on her own in New York City, I need to remember she can figure out whether or not to wear a winter coat.

Second, schedule fun together! Now that you have the time to check items off your bucket list, do it! Planning and anticipating fun activities and trips will draw you closer as a couple.

Finally, finish strong! Invest in younger marriages as you grow older, they need role models and you need to stay feeling young.

Life goes by fast, make every year count!

Thoughts: _____
_____
_____

Action Step: _____
_____

APRIL 28

"The road less traveled."

I saw a meme on Facebook that made me chuckle, and then just made me sad. It read:

"There's a Highway to Hell and a Stairway to Heaven... tells you something about traffic patterns, doesn't it?"

As Christians who are married and committed to the vow "til death do us part," we are on the road less traveled. We will be misunderstood, mocked, and ridiculed for honoring Christ and our vows to our spouse. However, when all is said and done we will reflect as was written in Frost's famous poem:

> *I shall be telling this with a sigh*
> *Somewhere ages and ages hence:*
> *Two roads diverged in a wood, and I--*
> *I took the one less traveled by,*
> *And that has made all the difference.*

So, fellow travelers, let's encourage one another to continue down this path together--in the end we will hear, "well done, thou good and faithful servant."

Thoughts: _____
_____
_____

Action Step: _____
_____

April 29

"See you later alligator."

When our daughter, Grace, was young we had this goodbye routine that we'd say every time Jay would leave the house. He' say, "See you later alligator!"

She replied, "After a while crocodile!"

And then I'd come back with, "If you're lucky rubber ducky!" And we'd give a kiss! It was a special time.

Hellos and goodbyes are special in your marriage too! While we wouldn't recommend the alligator banter, we would recommend a goodbye and a hello routine! Ours is very simple, we kiss every time.

One time, Laura was late and in a hurry for a meeting. She rushed out the door and started backing the car out of the garage. Just then, Jay walked out of the house and into the garage and stood there with his hands on his hips. She put the car into drive, sped back into the garage and swiftly kissed him goodbye.

See ya later alligator!

Thoughts: _____
_____
_____

Action Step: _____
_____

April 30

"Take the bull by the horns."

For our 10th anniversary, Jay had secretly scraped together just enough money to take a nice trip. He was working in youth ministry, so putting that kind of cash together was an accomplishment! On our anniversary he laid out the cash and some travel brochure in front of Laura and said, "take your pick!"

She immediately burst into tears, and not tears of joy. We had to have the hard conversation about Laura's credit card debt--but it did not lead to a fight! Jay simply took the money and a checkbook upstairs and helped fix the problem.

It was then that we took the bull by the horns and worked and scratched our way out of debt. We also took that 10 year anniversary trip--it was simply three years later when we'd paid off our debt and saved enough for the trip.

When the time comes in your marriage, don't be afraid to take the bull by the horns.

Thoughts: _____
_____
_____
_____

Action Step: _____
_____

May 1

"Under a microscope."

Once a year, it's important to put your marriage under a microscope. To take a long hard look at what's going well, and what could use improvement. We all have annual reviews at work, get our annual physical--hey, even New Year's Eve comes around every year!

It doesn't have to be a long, drawn-out process, but it will reap benefits. Go to dinner with the express purpose of discussing the highs and lows of the past year; come to the meal ready to share some of your highlights and some of the things that were disappointing. Discuss those together and make a plan for improvement.

Sound like too much work? Then find a marriage conference and let the facilitators help you along. There are many great marriage conferences google one near you and discover the benefit of investing in your marriage!

We hear couples all the time say that their annual getaway to a conference is actually a highlight of their year!

Thoughts: _____
_____
_____
_____

Action Step: _____
_____

May 2

"Variety is the spice of life."

Men can get by with just three of anything. Take pants for example: black pants, brown pants, and jeans; or shoes: black shoes, brown shoes, tennis shoes.

Ladies, on the other hand, fully understand and employ the notion that variety is the spice of life: I can't begin to count how many shoes Laura owns or how many personal hygiene items she has, our bathroom has drawers and drawers creams and lotions. It's overwhelming for the male brain.

Simply put, we are different! Men, for the most part, like the familiar--let's face it we all have that favorite shirt that we'll wear till it falls off our back.

Women, on the other hand love shiny new things. One of my friends calls herself a "crow" because she's attracted to shiny objects.

Whatever the case in your house, don't let the differences bug you, it's how God made us!

Thoughts: _____
_____
_____
_____

Action Step: _____
_____

May 3

Jay and I have been married for 31 years, travel the country helping people strengthen their marriage, and we still get marriage wrong from time to time.

We were doing a conference in Ft Wayne, Indiana, and during the soundcheck, things were not going well and we were both on edge. I said something to Laura that embarrassed her in front of the entire tech crew. She said, "Fine, you can do this conference on your own." I said, "Fine, it'll be better that way!"

Why is it so easy to hurt the one we love the most? Romans 3:23, "for all have sinned and fall short of the glory of God." That's the easy answer.

Why do we forgive when we are hurt? Because of Romans 3:24, "and all are justified freely by his grace through the redemption that came by Christ Jesus."

Oh and by the way, we kissed, made up, and had a great conference in Ft Wayne!

Thoughts: _____
_____
_____
_____

Action Step: _____
_____

May 4

"You can lead a horse to water but you cannot make him drink."

We get some of the most bizarre marriage questions emailed to our office. We answer every one but sometimes it takes us a few days to formulate the proper answer. However, usually the bottom line in every marriage is, are you going to do something about it?

Here's a riddle: five birds are sitting on a wire, one bird decides to fly away. How many are left? Five, because deciding to fly away, and flying away are two different things. The same is true in your marriage. You can decide you are going to work on your marriage, but until you actually do something, nothing will change.

In order to change, you must put yourself in a process. Join a small group or Bible study, seek counsel with a mentor couple, or read a book together.

As master Yoda once said to young Luke Skywalker "No think--do!"

Thoughts: _____
_____
_____
_____

Action Step: _____
_____

May 5

Life a little crazy right now? Seems like all of adult life is an adjustment--we learn to live single, then we learn to live married, then we learn to live with little ones, then with teens...then we learn to live as empty nesters. So what's the key to taming this crazy life?

Purpose -- When you know your purpose it allows you to say yes to the things you should be saying yes to and no to those things that do not help you achieve your purpose. Once you know your purpose, it helps you set your...

Priorities -- Establishing the people, ideas, and things that are important to you and the achievement of your purpose. Which all leads to your...

Propensity -- Toward creating habits that will lead you back to your purpose.

Want to tame this crazy life? It all starts with discovering your purpose.

Thoughts: _____
_____
_____
_____

Action Step: _____
_____

May 6

The weather is warm, flowers are blooming, it seems like the perfect setting and time for a wedding! Often, however, so much time is spent on the wedding at times we forget about the marriage that follows!

Start out right--what do you want your marriage to look like? As you look to the years ahead what do you want out of marriage? What are your dreams together? Now build that into your plans and habits.

In our 10th year of marriage, we were like hamsters on a wheel.... going a million miles an hour and getting nowhere! We sat down and asked ourselves what we wanted to be about as a couple. Asked and answered--we developed a mission statement for our marriage that gave us the foundation for our marriage to build upon. It isn't too late if you are already married!

In June, we want to encourage you with habits that healthy married couples build into their marriage.

Thoughts: _____
_____
_____
_____

Action Step: _____
_____

May 7

Having a grateful attitude is a healthy habit for your marriage.

Grateful as defined by dictionary.com as being thankful for what one has received. In marriage, in means being thankful for the spouse God has given you...even when you don't feel like it!

We can be honest here, there are days we don't like each other very much. I irritate him, he annoys me, it happens in every marriage. A healthy marriage has those moments, but moves past them and is reminded that God gave you each other to annoy, irritate, and love!

Having a grateful attitude isn't enough, we need to express our gratefulness as well!

Tell each other that you are thankful that you have each other. Let your spouse know how much you appreciate them with notes, texts, and your words.

We need to express gratefulness to our spouse, but also to God for the spouse He has given you! This is especially important to do on those days when you are irritated and or annoyed!

Thoughts: _____

_____

_____

Action Step: _____

_____

May 8

Ruth Bell Graham once stated "A happy marriage is the union of two good forgivers."

Boy isn't that the truth! And a truth we've had to practice over and over and over again. You see we're human, and as humans we make mistakes on a regular basis and some of those mistakes need forgiveness. But not just forgiveness--you see, happily married people also need to have short memories when it comes to being wronged. We have to forgive and forget.

Scripture gives us a great example to follow: Psalm 103:12 reads, "as far as the east is from the west, so far has he removed our transgressions from us."

When God forgives us, he has a short memory. He separates us from our sin as far as the east is from the west...just how far is that? Forever far. Let's follow his example! As Christ followers, we give our marriage the best when we forgive and forget!

Thoughts: _____
_____
_____

Action Step: _____
_____

May 9

We are big Detroit Lions fans! Every Sunday in the fall, whether at home or in an airport, you will find us planted in front of a TV, watching the Lions. We scream, we yell (unless in the airport), we cheer our Lions on!

A healthy married couple cheers each other on! We often say we are each other's biggest fan, Sometimes though, life comes along and we forget. Encouraging our spouse in the little things and the big things gives them confidence to go and do and be all that God has called them to be.

Laura just published her first solo book--a dream of hers since she was little. It was a 5 year process, and at times she wanted to give up and quit. Jay never let that happen. He cheered her on in those moments of giving up!

Be your spouse's biggest fan!

Thoughts: _____
_____
_____
_____

Action Step: _____
_____

May 10

We all have that perfect idealization of our marriage and our spouse in our head and hearts before we actually get married! Then we get married and, oops....that isn't what we thought!

I read once, "Strike an average between what a woman thinks of her husband a month before she marries him and what she thinks of him a year afterward, and you will have the truth about him in a very handy form." Realistic expectations are a habit of a healthy married couple. It is healthy to ask yourself what are fair expectations to hold for your spouse.

For instance, if a wife works until 5 pm every day it might not be a realistic for a husband to expect dinner to be ready at 5:30.

It is also unrealistic for a woman to expect her husband to come home from work and immediately be engaged in conversation with her. He needs some down time first! (at least most men I know do!)

Healthy couples have realistic expectations.

Thoughts: _____
_____
_____
_____

Action Step: _____
_____

May 11

We all know what a trust fall is, right? A trust fall involves standing of front of another person, your back to them, falling into their arms and completely trusting them to catch you. Healthy couples have that kind of complete trust in one another. A trust that says, I know when I fall you will be there to catch me. However, we know and understand that trust in marriage is at times broken. Through circumstances and bad decisions, trust no longer exists for a season.

Healthy couples also strive to earn and rebuild trust when it has been broken--understanding that it doesn't happen overnight but takes time.

It's like taking a sheet of paper today, and tomorrow placing another sheet of paper on the first one until, eventually, there will be a stack of paper. That is how trust is built (or rebuilt), one sheet of paper at a time.

Healthy couples completely trust and rebuild when it has been broken.

Thoughts: _____
_____
_____
_____

Action Step: _____
_____

MAY 12

Spirited conversations--I love this phrase! It means lively and vivacious.

Are the conversations in your home like that? Do you have the courage to say what needs to be said? Do you and your spouse enjoy lively conversation?

When it comes to disagreeing, we can also tend to be lively. The hardest aspect of disagreeing is finding the courage to say what needs to be said without hurting the other person.

Remember that if you love your spouse and value your marriage, you will have the courage to say the hard things in a loving way!

Healthy married couples have spirited conversations!

Thoughts: _____
_____
_____

Action Step: _____
_____

May 13

As men and women I think we inherently understand that we are different. We know it in our heads, but then when reality hits it's hard to comprehend just how different we are…it may be a whole new ball game!

We are so different! But guess what--that's okay! It is actually what adds spark to your marriage.

A favorite phrase in our marriage is, "If we were both the same, one of us wouldn't be necessary!"

I know which one, too! Healthy couples accept their differences. Rejoice in them and allow them to create a spark in your marriage!

Thoughts: _____
_____
_____

Action Step: _____
_____

May 14

As parents we've all heard a little one at one time or another ask the question--when are we going to arrive at our destination? They ask because they are tired of the journey.

All too often in marriage we have the same "destination" mentality because the journey can be rough at times. We begin to think, "I'll be happy when we have kids," "when they are out of diapers," "when they go to school," "when they go to college." Seeking a destination for your marriage keeps you from enjoying the journey.

What's the key to enjoying the journey? Being content.

Paul tells us in Philippians 4:12, "I have learned the secret of being content in any and every situation, whether well fed or hungry, whether living in plenty or in want."

So whether your journey right now has you living in plenty or in want, work to be content and realize the amazing path God has you walking today!

Thoughts: _____
_____
_____
_____

Action Step: _____
_____

May 15

When Jay and I decided to get married, we agreed together to never utter the "D" word. Divorce was not an option for us, therefore it would not even be in our vocabulary.

A healthy and happily married couple takes divorce off the table. They give themselves no out. They have an attitude of staying in for the long haul. It will be hard at times, but when we allow ourselves to think divorce is an option, it gives us permission not to do the hard work and just give up.

When those times of difficulty arrive in our marriage, we have 3 choices: be miserable, get out, or do the hard work. If we don't make divorce an option, we only have two options, and the choice becomes easier...do the hard work for your marriage!

Healthy married couples develop a habit of doing the hard work and don't allow divorce in their vocabulary.

Thoughts: _____
_____
_____

Action Step: _____
_____

May 16

When our kids were young ,the last thing we'd do before they left for school was hold hands in a circle and pray for our day. Laura being a cheerleading coach at the time, instead of saying "amen," we would all put hands in the middle of the circle and proclaim, "go-o-o-o, Jesus!"

We didn't do this disrespectfully, in fact quite the opposite--we were praising our Lord together as a family. It was a sign of unity.

What symbols of unity do you have in your marriage? For us, we always go to bed at the same time. We always disciplined our kids with both of us present. Obviously, our wedding rings were always a symbol.

So tonight, after the kids are in bed, ask your spouse about some ways that you two want to show the world and each other that you are a unified team.

Thoughts: _____
_____
_____
_____

Action Step: _____
_____

MAY 17

Traveling together is one of the healthiest things you can do for your marriage. We say it all the time, "get away and get ahead." There are so many benefits to traveling together as a couple.

First, it gives you an automatic discussion starter…"Where do we want to go next?" or, "Hey. look what I found for us to do while we're in the mountains."

Second, it builds anticipation. Anticipation is one of the most powerful emotions on the planet. Don't believe me? Just watch a child (or Laura for that matter) in the days and weeks before Christmas!

Finally, it gives the kids a break from mom and dad! You heard me right, one of the healthiest things you can do for your children is let them know that your relationship is a priority. A weekend at Grandma's or a trusted friend's home will give you and your kids a new appreciation for each other, and will keep your marriage strong!

Thoughts: _____
_____
_____
_____

Action Step: _____
_____

May 18

We encourage couples all the time to find something fun to do together. Add some fun to your marriage. One answer we hear time and time again is, "But Jay and Laura, we are not fun people!"

Healthy Couples enjoying activities together. It isn't about being fun it is about having fun...together!

Find things to do you both enjoy together! We love to cook together. This is something we enjoy doing year round. We enjoy golfing, running, and reading on the patio in the summer months...we are still looking for something other than napping that we enjoy in the winter!

Ask each other, what is something we can do together that we can both enjoy? Maybe it is hunting or fishing; maybe it is antiquing or fixing up your house. Find it and do it!

Thoughts: _____
_____
_____
_____

Action Step: _____
_____

May 19

When you were dating, phone calls, text messages, flowers, romantic dinners were all a part of the way you pursued your spouse. Then we get married, life happens, and the pursuing stops! We become too busy and we settle for complacency in our relationship.

A healthy couple will continue to pursue each other even in the midst of busy kids schedules and hectic lives. Is it easy? Nope, but it is necessary to keep your marriage healthy. Finding little ways to pursue your spouse.

This isn't rocket science--every night when Jay and I land in our chair to watch our favorite show, we always hold hands. It is that little touch that says I love you.

Maybe for you, it's leaving love notes around the house, or one on the dashboard of the car so your wife sees it as she takes the kids to school.

Whatever it is, make a plan and take the time to pursue your spouse.

Thoughts: _____
_____
_____
_____

Action Step: _____
_____

May 20

You've heard us say it before...Laura is skilled in sarcasm and Jay's love language is words of affirmation. Early in our marriage this was a huge issue, as Laura would use words to cut down rather than build up. And for someone whose love language is words of affirmation, it was like a double whammy. After we read Doctor Gary Chapman's book, the Five Languages of Love, I knew I had to "learn" how to communicate love to Jay in a way he understood.

Throughout marriage, it is important to continually communicate with your spouse about ways in which they do and do not affirm their love for you.

It's not always easy to confront an action or attitude that hurts our feelings but when we do we strengthen and build a richer deeper love for each other. And you'll have your spouse saying

"You are the one for me!"

Thoughts: _____
_____
_____
_____

Action Step: _____
_____

May 21

Whenever you buy a new car it comes with an owner's manual. And part of that manual is a maintenance schedule detailing when to get an oil change, rotate the tires, replace air filters, etc. Smart owners follow the schedule in order to keep their car in tip top shape!

Did you know there is an owner's manual for marriage? It's called the Song of Solomon, and it's packed full of practical advice for couples. For example, chapter 7, verse 11 says, "Come, my beloved, let us go to the countryside, let us spend the night in the villages."

If the Lord through His Holy Scripture encourages couples to get away together, don't you think smart couples would? This is just one example of many throughout the Song of Solomon which will help you strengthen your marriage.

Read Song of Solomon with your spouse then get out your calendar and schedule some much needed maintenance for your marriage!

Thoughts: _____
_____
_____

Action Step: _____
_____

MAY 22

Conversation involves both talking and listening. Healthy couples can do both!

When our son was 6, he busted me for not listening! He would come home from school and tell me all about his day, I would respond with, "uh huh," and, "mhm." I wasn't really listening, but was pretty sure he thought I was! One day, he switched it up on me and after a few minutes of telling me about his day, he asked me a question and I missed it! Busted!

Healthy conversation involves talking to your spouse and then listening to what they say. Often we are moving onto to the next thing we are going to say rather than listening to them!

An easy way to make sure you are listening is to repeat what your spouse said before you reply.

"So what you're saying is…" or, " what I hear you saying…"

Listen as well as talk…God gave us two ears and one mouth for a reason!

Thoughts: _____
_____
_____

Action Step: _____
_____

May 23

Facebook question:

"My husband and I have a blended family. It gets very difficult at times; we don't normally fight and argue But every other weekend, about the night before his son has to go back to his mom, we find ourselves fighting over the same issues we fought about two weeks before. Nothing gets resolved, it is swept under the rug and left alone to get bigger until the next time we have the argument. We are both tired of this. What do you suggest we do?"

Unfortunately, this happens all too often in blended families--especially when a child goes back and forth between homes.

Getting on the same page in your marriage with rules and boundaries for your home is the only way to solve the issue. It will take hard conversations and lots of give and take between husband and wife. But once you are on the same page, communicate this to all the kids

Blending takes time!

Thoughts: _____
_____
_____
_____

Action Step: _____
_____

May 24

"My husband and I were at one of your shows and thoroughly enjoyed it. You asked us to send you our questions, so here's mine. My husband recently connected with an old girlfriend from high school on Facebook. They've exchanged phone numbers and text and call each other. My husband claims there is nothing wrong with it. I feel differently. I feel like it just isn't right. Please help."

This is a great question and a very common issue for couples. We understand that Facebook is wonderful technology that lets us keep up with old friends and new. It can be a wonderful way to stay connected to people who are not close geographically.

Reconnecting with old girlfriends or boyfriends is a place we would highly recommend you draw the line. Connecting with old flames via Facebook, texting, calling or any other means is simply tempting fate. The chances of two people rekindling an old flame are just too high to risk this kind of interaction.

Thoughts: _____
_____
_____
_____

Action Step: _____
_____

May 25

I love the way Laura has learned to use words to encourage me. And of all the words she uses, these are some of the best: "Jay, I believe in you!"

When you say this to your husband, you are expressing your confidence in him and his future. It's almost like saying: "Honey, there is no person on this planet I would rather stand by, sit by, and sleep by than you."

One man put it this way: "My job responsibilities at work had been changed and I had been passed over for a promotion I'd been hoping for . . . She was there to encourage me and lift me up. She helped me understand it wasn't that there was anything wrong with me and that God had something better lined up."

And this wife commented: "When my husband wanted to start his business—leave the company he was with and go on his own—I told him I believed in him and he could do anything he put his heart into.

When a man knows his wife believes in him, he looks to the future with strength and optimism, unafraid to pursue his dreams.

Thoughts: _____
_____
_____

Action Step: _____
_____

May 26

There's a battle going on—and it's not just the fight in your kitchen or living room.

From unfulfilling jobs to overextended finances, to moral failures and unmet expectations, today's men engage daily in face-to-face combat. So when a wife intentionally says the words, "I believe in you," she often gives her man the courage he needs to slay the internal and external dragons he fights each day.

Here's one couple's story:

My husband started med school less than a month after we were married. When the stress or doubt would creep in, words became very powerful. Just knowing he had someone at home who believed in him and was waiting for him at the end of the day gave him strength. Simple words like "You can do this" when spoken by someone who loved him and believed in him reached his heart and helped him move forward.

The struggle is real for today's men, and as we wrestle to set and meet the right expectations, it means the world to know that our wives believe in us.

Thoughts: _____
_____
_____

Action Step: _____
_____

MAY 27

When you tell your husband "I believe in you"— It's a commitment to the direction and path the two of you have chosen to walk together. Yet for many men, life has tramped down their dreams far enough that they may no longer acknowledge them.

As a young man, I felt like a little boy, afraid to let others know what I truly wanted to do. Admitting I wanted to be on stage and speak seemed prideful. I thank God that for Laura, it seemed like a natural outflow of my God-given gifts and talents.

To help your husband unlock his God-given dream and potential, you might consider asking a few questions: What are you most passionate out? If money was no object, what would you do in life? Or what do you want future generations to remember you for?

Discovering your husband's dream might be the first step in communicating that you believe in him. So dare to dream together—and find a way to communicate "I believe in you" to your spouse today.

Thoughts: _____
_____
_____
_____

Action Step: _____
_____

May 28

When you tell your husband "I believe in you"—It's a commitment to the direction and path the two of you have chosen to walk together.

Yesterday, we encouraged you to believe in your husband by helping him to discover his dream. Today, we'd like to encourage you that as his wife, you also have the power to help him develop a dream for the two of you.

Working together as a team, ask this question: "If money was not an issue, what would we like our life to look like in 5 years?" Then work backward, creating measurable and attainable mini-goals to help you reach your vision.

When Jay and I decided to follow a four-year plan that would transition him out of his ministry job and into full speaking, we thought it would take four years. But through circumstances beyond our control, four years became four months. Trusting God for every aspect of our lives was scary, but also exhilarating.

So develop your plan, but keep in mind God may have a better one as the two of you develop your dream.

Thoughts: _____
_____
_____

Action Step: _____
_____

May 29

When you tell your husband "I believe in you"— It's a commitment to the direction and path the two of you have chosen to walk together.

Yesterday, we encouraged you to believe in your husband by helping him to develop a God-given dream. Today, we'd like to encourage you that as his wife, you also have the power to help him defend his dream.

When Jay dreamed of becoming a full-time speaker, we started a four-year plan that speeded up into a four-month one. The challenges can slow you down—or speed you up—but they don't have to throw you off course.

Often creativity is required—and in our case, Jay took a position with the public school system as a presenter of its curriculum and programs, conducting teacher in-service training. That left him free to travel on the weekends.

And in time, the dream became reality. Pray together about God's dream for you and seek Godly counsel. Once you commit to a dream and develop a plan, ask for God's leading in defending your dream against potential obstacles.

Thoughts: _____
_____
_____
_____

Action Step: _____
_____

May 30

Have you run across stinkin' thinking today? You know, self-centeredness that leads to manipulation, poor decisions, and me-first behavior. P.U.!

Henry Ford once said, "Thinking is the hardest work a man can do. That's why so few do it."

In Romans 12:1, Paul packs a punch when he urges us not to be conformed to the patterns of this world, but to be transformed by the renewing of our minds.

This is something only God can do in our marriages or otherwise: it's easy for our minds to get in a rut. Here's where God asks us to put away old ways of thinking about what makes up a solid marriage, and to seek from Him new and challenging thoughts about His will. And this is exactly what God can do in us when we surrender all of ourselves to him.

Colossians 3:1 says, "Since then, you have been raised with Christ, set your hearts on things above, where Christ is seated at the right hand of God." This is where stinkin' thinking gets left behind—when we embrace newness in Christ.

Thoughts: _____
_____
_____
_____

Action Step: _____
_____

May 31

What **will** we do today?

Use the word "will," and it's a reminder that we have a choice. God allows us to cooperate with him . . . so we can be transformed to be like Jesus. But if we're honest, many of us conform to the traits of our peers. Gratefully, our heavenly Father has more in mind for us and our marriages. It begins with the conforming of your will.

We witnessed its power with our friend Greg. Since he was always late, we told him an earlier time for dinner, hoping he would show up on time. His lack of punctuality frustrated his wife Sharon and everyone else. Until the day Greg willed himself to make a change. Greg drove himself to the store to buy a planner, and he actually used it. Over time, it became clear that Greg no longer missed meetings and appointments. He literally conformed his will.

The same principle works in marriage. We have the power to make right choices—conforming not to the world—but to the power of Christ alive in us.

Thoughts: _____
_____
_____

Action Step: _____
_____

June 1

"Jay, when was the last time you laid down your life for me?"

"When I ate the surprise mystery dish last week?"

All kidding aside, most of us know that Romans 12 invites us to "offer our bodies as living sacrifices, because this is our spiritual act of worship." When it comes to serving our spouses, we are to exemplify Christ's greatest challenge: "Greater love has no one than this, that he lay down his life for his friends."

And just when we start hemming and hawing about what that means, we are reminded in Philippians 2 that Jesus set the example—by laying down his life as a slave on our behalf. In marriage, we see that when we give up, when we do not have to win, we allow the Holy Spirit to work.

So when was the last time you laid down your life for your spouse? When was the last time you ignored your agenda to serve your family? As we serve, we are simply giving back the life that Christ has already given us.

Thoughts: _____
_____
_____
_____

Action Step: _____
_____

June 2

Laugh, rinse, repeat.

Jay and I had just moved into a new house, when we discovered that a neighbor's house had been burglarized. So naturally, I woke Jay up when I thought I heard an intruder. Grabbing my shotgun and slowly scouring the house, I turned on every light in the house. As I made my way back through the living room, I noticed car doors slamming at a neighbor's party and realized what had awoken Laura.

Now it was the neighbors turn to wake up. As Jay glanced out the window, he saw a woman on her porch staring, her eyes big as saucers. For not only was Jay holding a shotgun, he was buck naked in the middle of the living room—with all lights on.

Let's just say there was nothing to hide behind. Finally, I dropped to the floor and did the bugs bunny slither up the stairs.

We're still laughing about our marriage's funniest moments, because it lifts sorrow, diminishes arguments, and helps us survive almost anything. Have you had your laugh today?

Thoughts: _____
_____
_____
_____

Action Step: _____
_____

June 3

What provides an endorphin rush, brightens the mood, and may help your body heal itself? It's laughter. When it comes to marriage, and life in general, we've found laughter to be great medicine.

One year, I left our family to travel to Romania with some teens completing work projects in the city of Arad. At night, we met with Romanian teens for large meetings. As I presented Christ to these kids, I would start the evenings with a little comedy. Each night, a different teen would approach me to say, "Jay, I haven't laughed like that in my life!" What may have been a cliché to an American teen was the truth for the Romanian teens. Life was hard, and the healing power of laughter was unusual. In those moments, they learned what good medicine it can be!

The same is true in the dailyness of our marriages. Deep belly laughter releases powerful endorphins that soothe and comfort. So add some to your marriage today. Laughter makes good chemistry—and experience tells us it can make your marriage stronger.

Thoughts: _____
_____
_____
_____

Action Step: _____
_____

June 4

Anyone can laugh— But a person with a true sense of humor can laugh at him or herself!

Take Jay, for instance…one of his most irritating personal qualities, is his ability to laugh in the middle of an argument. We may be fussing and fuming and with no warning at all, a big grin comes across my face, a silly grin that makes it impossible for the other person not to smile.

"But I am in the middle of an argument," my brain says. "Don't grin." However, the war is over when Jay starts laughing. And then I start laughing. And suddenly I forgot what we were mad about in the first place.

If it's true that life is 90% what happens to me and 10% how I react to it, attitude can be a game-changer in marriage. That's why it helps to ask if the thing you're upset about will matter 100 years from now. If not, considering how stepping back and laughing at yourselves might change the moment. Not to mention creating some great memories.

Thoughts: _____
_____
_____
_____

Action Step: _____
_____

June 5

Martin Luther once said: "I judge the depth of a man's faith by his ability to laugh."

When the problems of marriage overwhelm, faith is always required—and laughter may be, too. Yes, there will be issues only solved through hard work and a faith that God can transport you to the other side of the problem. Other times, a sense of humor will be what is needed to put life together in perspective.

Imagine yourself in the middle of a storm, with thunder, lightning, and howling wind. Rain is coming down so hard you can't see your hand. Suddenly, you are startled to see a picture of yourself. Your hair is plastered to your head, your mascara running, just as your wet shirt sleeves began to hang down over your hands. And now the storm has lost its ability to terrify you.

Laughter in the middle of stormy arguments can give you a broader perspective: you may find the issue has lost its power. The storm may not be gone; but the way you see it is.

Thoughts: _____
_____
_____
_____

Action Step: _____
_____

June 6

In Proverbs 4:23, Solomon reminds us, "Above all else, guard your heart, for it is the wellspring of life."

Have you ever wondered what life would be like without emotions? The emotions in our hearts drive, motivate, and prod us to interact with the world around us. That's why we're encouraged to guard our hearts—because life starts here.

In families, we are also responsible to help guard the hearts of our spouse and children. This principle plays out with our good friends Gene and Wendy, and their daily journey through married life. Gene's sense of humor is drier than unbuttered toast, and sometimes people don't know when he's joking around. Wendy's a kind, considerate woman, who happens to be Gene's biggest fan. When he starts cracking jokes, Wendy splits her gut with laughter! Even when we can't tell if Gene is joking, the rest of us laugh along, because Wendy's laughter is so contagious.

Laughter literally reaches deep within us and changes our hearts. So why not spend some time recalling funny moments in your marriage today?

Thoughts: _____
_____
_____

Action Step: _____
_____

June 7

Some people turn to caffeine for a pick-me-up. But when it comes to emotional energy in a marriage, no amount of high-octane coffee can replace an empty emotional tank.

Our friend Bill understood this, after marrying at age 42 and then having three children within three years. "I've realized it's not about time," Bill said. "It's about how much emotional energy I have saved for my family when I come home at the end of the day."

These days, it's hard to work in any kind of business without giving a lot of yourself. As a result, it's common to come home with nothing left to give to the people who need our emotional energy the most. In the end, Bill made a better choice: "I have had to learn to keep a reserve of emotional energy so that when I come home, I'm not just physically present but I'm engaging with them as well."

To maintain emotional intimacy with your spouse will take prioritizing, committing, and often turning off the TV and computer. And the rewards are worth it!

Thoughts: _____
_____
_____

Action Step: _____
_____

June 8

Husband and wives around the country are discovering how to nurturing emotional intimacy—one conversation at a time.

One woman reported:

"I am learning to think before speaking and not say the first thing that enters my mind. I need to be gentler with my words . . . less defensive . . . so that my husband will want to hear me."

To enter these vulnerable emotional waters, we have to let our emotions show.

One night, Jay and I were watching a police drama on TV. This episode dealt with homeless mothers and children. At the conclusion of the show, I looked at my normal, masculine husband and saw tears streaming down his face. He laughed a little as he wiped his tears. As for me, his vulnerability was an attractor for me.

It's just one example of how Jay and I continue to build emotional intimacy. As you show interest and safety when your spouse shows emotion, you reinforce the promise you made to cherish each other in every way.

Thoughts: _____
_____
_____

Action Step: _____
_____

June 9

The American Psychological Association reports that 40-50% of today's marriages end in divorce. (http://www.apa.org/topics/divorce/) Often happily-ever-after becomes happy-no-more.

Although no one can guarantee a marriage that's divorce-proof… It takes two to tango after all…here's something that often helps a couple weather storms in a marriage.

When I was 16, my mom and I were doing dishes. I knew mom and dad were going through a stretch of rough water. So after we finished, I asked my mother if she and Dad were going to get a divorce. Almost before the words got out of my mouth, she had swatted me upside the head with the dish towel! She responded to my questions in these words, "Jay, if there is one thing I know, it is that your father and I will never get a divorce. You see, son, your dad loves Jesus even more than he loves me."

No matter the state of your marriage today, settle one thing in your heart. Commit to loving Jesus more than you love your spouse. And ask for his help in strengthening your marriage bond.

Thoughts: _____

_____

_____

_____

Action Step: _____

_____

June 10

It may not seem easy to measure the spiritual temperature of your home. There's no thermometer for that!

But it's often obvious. When she was five, our daughter understand she was a spiritual being, that there was something bigger out there. One Sunday our pastor preached a sermon reminding us that in the cosmos we are nothing but dust. After he prayed, "Oh, Lord, even though we are nothing but dust…" Grace leaned over and said, "Daddy, what's butt dust?"

In Matthew 18, the words of Jesus tell us something about the true spiritual temperature of our home. He says that whatever we bind on earth will be bound on heaven, and whatever we loose will be loosed in heaven as well. And that if we agree on something, our heavenly Father wants to do that for us.

For married couples, this reminds us that God hears us when we pray with our spouse, that if we release destructive habits in Jesus' name, he wants to empower us to let them go. And that he is always with us.

Thoughts: _____
_____
_____

Action Step: _____
_____

June 11

What if someone offered you a life of unspeakable joy? Jesus said "I have come that they might have life, and that they might have it to the full." Is your marriage full of that abundant life?

It's easy for a spouse to say, at least we're doing well spiritually. But going to church together isn't necessarily an indicator of abundant life. All of the areas of our life and hearts flow together—spiritually, physically, mentally, and emotionally. Make sure you're pursuing true wholeness in your marriage, not an "institutional relationship with Jesus." Truthfully, the only way to do this is to rely on God's power to open up intimacy in all areas of your marriage.

We lay our marriage down when we pray: "It's not about my desires, needs or expectations. Lord, take my spouse and make him or her into the partner I need, and Lord, take and make me into the partner my spouse needs." As you yield to God, he delights in moving in your marriage to grow your joy and unity, one prayer at a time.

Thoughts: _____
_____
_____
_____

Action Step: _____
_____

JUNE 12

The eyes of engaged couples often glaze over when told that marriage takes work. I wouldn't have believed it myself when Laura and I first met. As we took in a baseball game, Laura grabbed my hand, and I felt my heart leap out of my chest. At first I was so shocked that I thought it was the hot dogs coming back up… But later I would inform Jay that this was actually "love." My insides wanted to explode with joy. You can probably remember a similar moment with your spouse.

In 5, 10, or 15 years, however, the excitement fades. You realize you have to work at this thing called marriage. Too bad no one prepared you up front. This is when your commitment means you choose to say "I Do" to the concept of marriage over and over again.

Accepting that marriage takes work starts with the full acceptance that your spouse is all you need. You don't need a new model. God, in his grace, gives us years to perfect loving the one we're with.

Thoughts: _____
_____
_____

Action Step: _____
_____

June 13

News Flash: God didn't create marriage as a problem to be fixed— But as a beautiful union of two human beings who might explore life together. Before God created marriage, he designed the land and sea, the plants and trees, the sun and stars. Then the fish, the birds, and the animals. Finally, he created man.

In Genesis 1, God calls all the creation good. The he creates Adam. And I personally think he said, "I can do one better," then created Eve. It wasn't until both humans were created that God called it all "very good."

In a world without heavy expectations, I doubt Adam ever wondered if Eve was all he needed. And I'm not sure Eve thought she had to train Adam to be a better husband. It was obvious they were made for each other.

This type of closeness and intimacy requires trust in a God who created both you and your spouse, knows you, and longs for you to say "I do" to a marriage filled with passion, closeness, and desire.

Thoughts: _____
_____
_____
_____

Action Step: _____
_____

June 14

What 7 things does your wife need every single day? Don't worry, it's easier than you think. She needs seven significant touches that are given without expectation—touches that make her feel desired and loved.

To communicate your care for the woman in your life, start by:

- being intentional; slow down enough to initiate things like holding her hand, putting your arm around her shoulder, or rubbing her back as she cooks dinner

- realizing that a non-sexual touch can include calling her during work to see how her day is going, picking up a loaf of bread or some flowers, or even emailing her. That's right!

By the time dinner arrives, it's more than possible to have already given your wife 5 significant non-sexual touches that let her know she matters to you.

The truth is, when it comes to showing your wife she matters to you, it really is about the little things. So starting right now, see if you can give her the 7 significant touches that will make her feel loved today.

Thoughts: _____

_____

_____

Action Step: _____

_____

June 15

Yesterday we talked about the 7 significant touches your wife needs every day to know you love and appreciate her. Today, we'd like to share a few stories from husbands and happy wives:

- One day while she was at work I cleaned the house from top to bottom. Did all the laundry and had supper on the table when she got home, complete with a rose and a note that said "I miss you."

- One wife says, "He tells me all the time. By brushing my shoulder whenever he walks past me, praying with me in the morning, snuggling with me after a hard day, and listening to my struggles with clients. He comes up behind me and puts his arms around me and kisses me on my neck.

- Another says, "It's the little things...touching my back as he walks by, the way he holds my face in his hands when he kisses me, the way he holds on so tight when we hug.

Husbands, you have the power to love your wife today with 7 significant touches.

Thoughts: _____
_____
_____
_____

Action Step: _____
_____

June 16

We often tell couples that women need 7 significant, non-sexual touches a day. What we don't always mention is that guys actually benefit from the same. So in all seriousness, ladies—stop right now, and go hug your man!

Stereotypes often label women as the ones who want affectionate touching. But the truth is both men and women crave it, according to an article on self-growth.com. The authors claim that once men experience affectionate touch, they love to be touched in this way as well. Quote "such caresses help break through times of low self-esteem, fear, and doubt…"

Jay has his own way of showing me how he likes to be loved. After my daughter and I returned home from a shopping trip, he greeted us at the door with a smile, warm hugs, and an elaborate welcome. When I told him how nice it was, he replied "I would love to be greeted that way too when I come home from a guys' only golf trip."

Ladies, a tender hug or a gentle pat can go a long way.

Thoughts: _____

_____

_____

_____

Action Step: _____

_____

June 17

Billy Joel once sang, "I love you just the way you are…" To which Jay Laffoon replied, "Yeah, right!"

Our conversations with couples around the country reveal that many of us would like to change some things in our spouses.

The women's survey revealed they wished men would:

- not try to solve our problems for us, but just listen
- improve listening skills
- listen more attentively & open up more

The guys said they wish women would:

- complain less
- criticize less
- nag less
- and judge less

Well, at least we're all talking about communication! But what's happening here? When a man doesn't listen well, a woman doesn't feel respected or loved.

When a woman complains and nags, a man doesn't feel his wife is ever proud of him.

These general trends reveal how often we miss each other in our conversations—and how we can do better when it comes to genuine, loving communication.

Thoughts: _____

_____

_____

_____

Action Step: _____

_____

June 18

Make time for affection and intimacy with your spouse. Check!
Schedule time to plan and have fun together. Check!
Spiritually connect with your spouse. I'd LIKE to!

When it comes to spiritually intimacy, our personal survey shows it's often a struggle.

Our survey revealed three main spiritual detractors in a marriage:

- A spouse who is overly involved at church and has no time;
- Believing spouses who do not share service or prayer;
- Or a spouse who does not share your faith.

Those whose spouse doesn't share their faith often make a decision to love as Christ loves, to faithfully pray for their spouse, and to remain committed to both their spouse and their heavenly Father.

For the rest of us, we may need to say "no" to good things so we can say "yes" to growing spiritually with our spouse. Look for common areas where you can serve, rather than going it alone. And find common ground where you can grow in approaching God together, through prayer, Bible study, or service. Look for ways to make it happen this week.

Thoughts: _____
_____
_____
_____

Action Step: _____
_____

June 19

Burger King says "have it your way."
"Loreal says, "You're worth it."
Many of us spend the first 20 years of our lives being told, "It's all about you!"

Get your education....Get your job...Get your spouse...and fulfill YOUR needs.

To the contrary, Colossians 3:5 reminds us, "Put to death, therefore, whatever belongs to your earthly nature." We are to literally die to our self-centeredness. When we stood at the altar and said "I do" to our spouse, we became one instead of two, relinquishing our selfishness. We become not just Jay and Laura, but one—representing the marriage of Jay and Laura.

Though Laura's a natural sleeper, she made a decision as our kids were growing up to get up early enough to wake them. She put aside her desire to sleep because she wanted to give that part of herself for the sake of our family. And truthfully, she also wanted the children's clothing to match!

When we embrace the value and worth God places on us, it becomes easier to lose our self-interest so we can selflessly love others.

Thoughts: _____
_____
_____
_____

Action Step: _____
_____

June 20

Elizabeth Barrett Browning wrote, "How do I love thee? Let me count the ways…"

Do you believe there are endless ways you can love your spouse? Though the way we love varies from marriage to marriage, It all starts with this question:

"What am I doing every day to show my spouse that he or she is my priority?" Be assured that when you prioritize your spouse, you will give up something in the process. It's all part of the journey to becoming one.

Though most of us look forward to days off on the weekend, Jay is usually gone. So he clears his schedule on Mondays to accompany me to the grocery store. On his day off, he chooses to invest in our marriage while we walk up and down the food aisles. This is an example of doing something for our relationship instead of only thinking of himself.

Take a moment to ask yourself today, what am I doing to show my spouse he or she is my priority?

Thoughts: _____

_____

_____

Action Step: _____

_____

June 21

Jay and I want to encourage you to heat up your marriage daily—with intentional hellos and goodbyes.

I witnessed the power of my grandparents kissing each other each time grandpa left. He was skinny and 6'2" tall, bending down to my grandma, full-figured and 4'10" tall. They embraced and kissed each other when granddad left on long trips in his truck, or when he would be gone for 5 minutes to the grocery store. Pop taught me that every kiss a man gives a woman is important.

All of those kisses made an impact because they communicated intimacy. And the warmth of a welcome at the end of the day is just as important—it reminds both spouses of the bond they share, in and outside the bedroom.

It will take a few more minutes in the morning and at the end of the workday, but greeting your spouse with a passionate kiss and embrace communicates a warmth that keeps a marriage intimate, thriving…and strong.

Thoughts: _____
_____
_____
_____

Action Step: _____
_____

June 22

It's hard to believe, but . . . . Jay can literally lift me up or drag me down into the weeds by his tone of voice. Oh, the power!

But seriously, our marriage has opened my eyes to how voice inflections have the power to heal or destroy. For example, when I say, "I suppose…" [put an emphasis on the "ose" and a sigh at the end] this is really not the enthusiastic answer Laura hopes for when she wants to go the mall. Hardly! So the words I use have different meanings depending on the tone I say them with.

Together, we've found over and over again that using a tone affirming the other leads to communication that breeds happiness and harmony—instead of sulking and passive-aggressive cycles.

Does your tone communicate something damaging to your spouse? The cure is crying out for God's help and choosing a tone of voice that begins to communicate love, honor, and respect. Tending to your tone can reap major dividends in building a marriage that lasts.

Thoughts: _____
_____
_____
_____

Action Step: _____
_____

June 23

"Laura, what do women want?" "They want it all!"

Inside our book, He said, She Said, Jay and I have uncovered 4 powerful things a wife needs to hear from her husband. One of those winning phrases women long to hear is:

I cherish you.

What are the magic ways a woman just knows her husband treasures her for who she is? Simple things like sharing his life with her, thinking of no one else but her, and communicating that he both desires AND needs her in his world.

Got it…a wife needs to know she is cherished—and it starts when she feels loved, respected, and desired. When a man needs his wife, nurtures her, and is tender with her, he communicates to her and the world: "I have forsaken all others for her!"

We can't say the words "I cherish you" or "I treasure you" are magic words, but we do know they foster healing, joy, and mutual love and respect in most marriages. Try them today. You might be surprised at the power of these winning words.

Thoughts: _____

_____

_____

Action Step: _____

_____

June 24

"Jay, what do men want?" "Do you really want me to answer that?" Kidding aside, one of the top four things husbands need to hear is: "I'm proud of you!"

One day I was leaving on a ministry trip. Little did I realize Jay was desperately longing to hear the words I said that day: "I'm proud of you!"... As I entered the airplane, I was a crying, blubbery, snotty-nosed mess. I'm sure other passengers wondered if I was OK. Even I was shocked at how hungry I was to hear these words from my wife. She sent me on my way with a full and confident heart.

Ladies, these words are like gold to your husband, and they are easy to use. Just say, "I'm proud of the ways you . . . then fill in the blank.

Now I've learned these words mean even more to Jay during times of crisis and when I say them in front of others. So try them today. You might be surprised at the power of these winning words.

Thoughts: _____
_____
_____

Action Step: _____
_____

June 25

Have you noticed this about couples you meet? Often one tends to be more punctual than the other.

"Laura!! Your hair was fine 5 minutes ago!"

Growing up, my father often said these words: "Jay, if you're five minutes early, you're on time. If you're on time, you're late." Years later, Jay's father would explain that if you're always late, you tell others your time is more valuable than yours. "Son, he said, "That is just plain rude."

Sadly, we communicate the same thing to our spouse by constantly keeping them waiting. If you want to live a life and nurture a marriage that points people to Christ, consider working with your spouse to honor each other by helping each other be on time. Two really are better than one, when both encourage the other to develop strategies that help them to wisely manage their time.

So team up with your spouse to create enough margin in your schedule to be on time. Your efforts will help you redeem the hours and days you've been given—for everyone's benefit.

Thoughts: _____
_____
_____
_____

Action Step: _____
_____

June 26

Women are like crockpots. Men are like microwaves. We're discussing kitchen appliances to help heat up your marriage at a time when many couples are thinking about intimacy.

To be specific, husbands are often thinking of intimacy in the bedroom, while wives are often dreaming of all of the affection and tenderness that comes before it. We know how easy it is to get frustrated when your husband or wife has different needs and expectations for your relationship.

So let's begin the cooking process by remembering this:

Men, a woman usually needs to be plugged in in the morning and to be reminded of your love throughout the day, so remember to cherish her to keep her on a low simmer throughout the day.

And ladies, a man is often ready for intimacy in the bedroom at any time. Connect with and communicate with your spouse to build your desire. Surprise him with your interest. Think of him and remember what it is that made you desire him in the first place. Now, get cooking!

Thoughts: _____
_____
_____

Action Step: _____
_____

June 27

"Jay, can we go to lunch?"
"Not now, Laura. I'm in the middle of something."

This was a regular occurrence in some of our first years of marriage. Let's try this again. "Jay, can we go to lunch?"

"Uh, sure honey. I'd love to. Just give me 5 minutes."

In those growing-up-in-our marriage years, Jay learned that my love language is Quality Time. I needed Jay's presence and companionship to feel loved. What I didn't need was exactly what Jay did need. Physical touch.

Thank goodness that over time we discovered each other's love language. I stopped trying to love Laura the way I wanted to be loved and loving her through Quality Time. And I stopped treating Jay as if Quality Time was all he needed to be loved—offering backrubs, hand-holding, and physical affection as the gift he was wired to receive.

To discover your spouse's love language, read The 5 Languages of Love by Dr. Gary Chapman. Expressing the right love language to your spouse helps create a purposeful, thriving marriage that goes the distance, no matter what comes.

Thoughts: _____
_____
_____
_____

Action Step: _____
_____

June 28

When was the last time you had fun with your spouse? Before marriage, we tend to find plenty of ways to "play" together. Attending sporting events and concerts, going for hikes outdoors, enjoying a special movie or event that your significant other enjoys.

So why does saying "I do" often mean we begin to say "I don't" to the fun activities that brought us together in the first place?

The cure for a marriage without fun involves 3 things: 1) spend time communicating with your spouse about what activities each of you find joy in; 2) intentionally prioritize and schedule those activities on your official calendar; and 3) just do them!

The philosopher Plato said you can learn more about someone through an hour of play than through an hour of talking.

If that's true, you might be on the verge of discovering some amazing things about your spouse when you make the time to play together. "Laura, can we go golfing?" "Sure, honey, right after we go to the mall!" Couples that play together do tend to stay together.

Thoughts: _____
_____
_____
_____

Action Step: _____
_____

June 29

Have you experienced the power of positive affirmation?

For example, when kids hear "no" all of the time, they can internalize negativity. In contrast, a parent who also offers positive affirmation can often redirect a child. "Johnny, I love the way you helped mom out today. Let's do that again." We may not be kids anymore, but no spouse wants to hear "no" all of the time. Instead, we can open our minds to the power of yes.

If you find yourself saying "no" often, consider questions like these: "Honey, do you think we would enjoy going to ...this place...together on Saturday?" "Honey, what would be a way we could communicate about finances where neither one of us would get frustrated?" Too many nos are a warning sign that spouses may be expecting too much or too little, or that communication has broken down.

Find a solution by working on ways in which you can say yes to your spouse and to your marriage. Positive affirmation holds the power to deepen your love and respect for each other, starting today.

Thoughts: _____
_____
_____

Action Step: _____
_____

June 30

It's time for our heart checkup. 1 Corinthians 13, the love chapter, says:

> Love is patient, love is kind. It does not envy, it does not boast, it is not proud. It does not dishonor others, it is not self-seeking, it is not easily angered, it keeps no record of wrongs.
>
> Love does not delight in evil but rejoices with the truth. It always protects, always trusts, always hopes, always perseveres.

Whatever your expectations for love, 1 Corinthians 13 can help to reshape, realign, and transform them.

So how's your heart? Because love isn't something to celebrate once a year. Our assignment as spouses is to build love everyday. Instead of expecting the moon from your spouse today, consider this: How can you patiently love your spouse today, seeking their best? How can you overlook an offense? How can you protect, hope, and persevere in your marriage?

1 Corinthians 13 reminds us that love never fails. That's something we need to celebrate and live out in our marriages every day of the year.

Thoughts: _____
_____
_____
_____

Action Step: _____
_____

July 1

Is your marriage a contract? Or a covenant?

Simply signing a marriage license and saying vows doesn't make your marriage more than a contract. While making your marriage legal is important, there are layers of connection that can only be experienced when both partners consider their marriage to be a covenant.

No, making your marriage a covenant goes much deeper—to the level of your hearts. What did you intend when you said "I do"? What do you intend even now as you nurture, fight for, and grow a marriage that honors each other and God?

Here's an example: In the Bible, our covenant-making God made a covenant with Abraham, promising to make him "the father of many nations." And God came through on his promise.

When you say "I do" to your spouse, and you intend it as a covenant, you imply that you will honor and uphold your side of the marriage. You make the covenant before God, believing he will be right in the middle of it.

Find out more and sign a pledge at covenantmarriage.com.

Thoughts: _____
_____
_____

Action Step: _____
_____

July 2

I heard once that men are like waffles with compartments. And women are like spaghetti with everything mixed together. (Thank you Bill and Pam Farrell!) While this tends to make me think of Jay in a giant waffle costume….it only tends to make me think I'm hungry for either waffles or spaghetti!

But truthfully, we've become convinced that God doesn't compartmentalize our lives or our marriages. What grows us spiritually closer to God ACTUALLY DOES grow us to become more intimate with our husband or wife.

Let me give you an example. To pray together is an act of great intimacy. One night at our Bible study, each person prayed and thanked God out loud for specific things about their spouse, even though it felt awkward. Afterward, I noticed the couples connecting and cuddling.

And no wonder. Prayer is an intimate act that is a great attractor to spiritual intimacy with your spouse.

So try it today. Brief times of prayer with your spouse—or even praying alone for your spouse— can keep the spark in your marriage alive day-in-and-day-out.

Thoughts: _____
_____
_____

Action Step: _____
_____

July 3

On this Day before Independence Day as we prepare to celebrate our country… We'd like to declare it "Interdependence" Day.

Dictionary.com defines interdependence as "the quality or condition of being interdependent, or *mutually reliant on each other.*" What a great word for marriage! The truth is, so-called wedded bliss is never blissful without it!

We believe very couple can enjoy the spiritual blessings of interdependence by participating in 4 blessings found in Ecclesiastes 4.

Blessing One: "Two are better than one, because they have a good return for their labor" (v. 9 NIV).

Laura and I say we have one brain between the two of us. It may not be true for everyone, but after 31 years of marriage—we find that we do our best work when we work together. We see things from different perspectives—and that allows us to see the entire picture when facing a challenge. That's why we believe working together on your marriage can bring a "good return for your labor."

Time to wish your spouse a "happy Interdependence Day!"

Thoughts: _____
_____
_____
_____

Action Step: _____
_____

July 4

While we celebrate Independence Day and the privilege of living in a free country. . . We're celebrating the beauty of interdependence in marriage.

Dictionary.com defines interdependence as "the quality or condition of being interdependent, or *mutually reliant on each other*." What a great word for marriage!

See if you recognize this blessing of interdependence, found in Ecclesiastes 4:10: "If either of them falls down, one can help the other up. But pity anyone who falls and has no one to help them up" (v. 10).

One winter, I contracted pneumonia. I slept all week so I could travel the next weekend for our Ultimate Date Night shows. Gratefully, Laura took care of everything around the house. She handled both her weekly duties and mine. There is no doubt in my mind that without her help, I would not have been able to keep my commitments each weekend.

Today, thank God for the beauty of interdependence in marriage, and dream about ways you and your spouse can "help each other up," come what may.

Thoughts: _____

_____

_____

_____

Action Step: _____

_____

July 5

While we celebrate Independence Day this week and the privilege of living in a free country. . . We're celebrating the beauty of interdependence in marriage.

Dictionary.com defines interdependence as "the quality or condition of being interdependent, or *mutually reliant on each other.*" What a great word for marriage. And a good reminder that when two become one, it's not so they can both go it alone!

See if you recognize this blessing of interdependence, found in Ecclesiastes 4, verse 11: "...if two lie down together, they will keep warm. But how can one keep warm alone?" (v. 11).

How indeed!

While this passage certainly applies to cold winter nights—(and maybe not so much summer ones)—we also think it suggests the importance of having someone alongside you through the "cold days" life can throw at us, which have nothing to do with the weather. A spouse can speak encouraging words during tough times. A spouse can remind another spouse of God's faithfulness in the past. And sometimes just being there, being "alongside," is enough—no words are necessary.

Thoughts: _____

_____

_____

_____

Action Step: _____

_____

July 6

While we celebrate Independence Day this week and the privilege of living in a free country. . . We're celebrating the beauty of interdependence in marriage.

Dictionary.com defines interdependence as "the quality or condition of being interdependent, or *mutually reliant on each other.*" What a great word for marriage. And a good reminder that when two become one, it's not so they can both go it alone!

See if you recognize this blessing of interdependence, found in Ecclesiastes 4, verse 12: "Though one may be overpowered, two can defend themselves. A cord of three strands is not quickly broken."

When we stand together, whether the issue relates to the kids or a life decision, we can stand strong. And when Christ is at the center of our relationship, it makes us even stronger. He is the third strand. Keeping Christ as the focal point of any marriage does not mean hardship will not come—but it does mean you and your spouse will have the strength to fight the battle.

Thoughts: _____
_____
_____
_____

Action Step: _____
_____

July 7

Help! When your marriage or life hits a crisis, where will you and your spouse go to communicate?

Growing up, we had one bathroom for a family of four. But today, spouses often have a separate bathroom for themselves and one for their kids. This explains how Laura and I routinely found our bathroom to be a place to discuss private issues that were inappropriate for little ears.

Like the time Jay's mother was diagnosed with cancer—and we used our bathroom to discuss, weep, and plan how to handle the situation.

Of course, your marriage might include any number of issues you need to discuss privately: job difficulties, family issues, financial concerns, church problems, or surprise family activities.

Whatever the case, even if it's a closet or a car, find your sacred space to hash out the world's problems together so you can face them as a united team.

Then choose how much you want your children to hear, being honest and open with them after you've had your time to process. There are wise ways to communicate through crisis.

Thoughts: _____
_____
_____
_____

Action Step: _____
_____

July 8

Got spiritual intimacy in your marriage?

Taking the spiritual temperature of a couple isn't as easy as church attendance or praying together. We each long for a union that incorporates mental, physical, emotional, and spiritual intimacy. And we've found you can't have the latter without the former.

But we have found a sure path to connection and oneness. It's the biblical concept of confessing our weaknesses to one another.

Proverbs 28:13 says, "He who conceals his sins does not prosper, but whoever confesses and renounces them finds mercy."

On the winding road to nurturing spiritual intimacy with Jay, I discovered a nagging struggle with selfishness. Whatever I thought Jay "got," I wanted more of. While Laura was realizing and confessing her struggle with selfishness, I uncovered my own hidden agenda: I wanted things my way, and only my way. I demanded much from Laura without understanding the load she was carrying.

When we confessed our sins to each other, the Holy Spirit unleashed a power in our marriage that continues today. Confession is good for the soul—and for a marriage.

Thoughts: _____

_____
_____
_____

Action Step: _____

_____

July 9

"Why can't my spouse express emotions like me?"

The answer is easy: "Because they're not you. And that's a good thing!"

Riding the emotional rollercoaster in a marriage takes energy, understanding, and an ability to laugh.

One day, Laura heated up some delicious chili for our lunch, and even prepared the table for a simple romantic lunch.

Even though I am the one whose emotions went topsy-turvy after age 40....

I was the one who took one bite of the chili, realized it was too hot, and shoved the whole bowl off the table, exclaiming: "What are you trying to do, kill me?" "Are you just going to sit there?!?" was my next line...until I began to see how I ignored Laura's thoughtfulness simply because my chili was too hot.

Jay's overreaction not only ruined his lunch; it took some time to restore our emotional intimacy. Remember, the grace you extend for your spouse's emotional reactions is the same grace you will need . . . the next time he or she overheats the chili.

Thoughts: _____
_____
_____

Action Step: _____
_____

July 10

Every relationship we have will journey through 4 stages.

The honeymoon stage is when you are head over heels in love and forgiveness comes easy. *I adore you!*

The chaos stage is often when children are born and routines become solid. *Those habits of yours? They're…interesting.*

But we must push through to the third stage to be "emptied" so we can truly serve our spouse and our marriage. *I see life isn't all about me…at all!*

And only then will we achieve the fourth stage: unity. *Finally, we're working together. All for one, and one for all!*

We saw the beauty of this firsthand, when my mom entered rehabilitation, and my dad made it his job to serve mom and her needs. And the more he served, emptying himself, the more he became like Christ.

But what keeps couples from moving forward? Inevitably, it's pride. Movement happens when we choose to empty ourselves as Christ did, taking the position of a servant. The more we empty ourselves, the more room there is within us for Him.

Thoughts: _____
_____
_____
_____

Action Step: _____
_____

July 11

Do you worship God with your body?

Romans 12:1 asks us to submit our bodies to God as living sacrifices . . .

Sacrifices that are holy and acceptable to him. We all know that we worship God by gathering in church communities, studying his word, through prayer, and in fellowship with others.

But imagine my surprise in college when a professor pointed out that when a husband and wife are intimate, they are engaging in the ultimate form of worship, through their bodies!

In this act, we mysteriously offer ourselves to God, reflecting his power, majesty, and love.

When we offer our bodies to our spouses, and Christ is at the center of our marriage, this is an act of worship—a reflection of the God who is three in one. Otherwise known as a little bit of heaven on earth.

This is one powerful and beautiful way we worship God through our marriages, and that's a great reason to celebrate it. As we seek to keep our marriages holy, God honors the altar in our bedroom.

Thoughts: _____
_____
_____
_____

Action Step: _____
_____

July 12

Who said: "I am not a mind reader!" Every husband on the planet!

In the "he said, she said" world of marriage, there are some things a husband needs to hear. One of those is: I need you to [blank].

While we've found it to be true that what a wife needs often changes from day-to-day, we've found that husbands consistently need clear, concise communication.

Men don't tend to get hints. And to be blunt, we're often completely oblivious to what women think of as obvious.

The truth is, a woman's senses are more acute than a man's, and her brain can more freely move information from left to right in her brain.

Enter "woman's intuition"—and the desperate need I have for Laura to say not "the trash is full" but "Jay, would you please take out the trash?"

Ladies: Simple, direct, complete sentences are best. And they help us avoid scenarios where the wife asks, "Is this your underwear on the floor?" And the husband says: "It better be!" The truth is we simply think and process information differently.

Thoughts: _____
_____
_____

Action Step: _____
_____

July 13

Few things bring me more joy than helping my wife solve a problem. Just like Larry the Cable Guy, when it comes to helping their wives and children, most men want to "get 'er done!" But we can't "get 'er done" if our wives don't use specific, concise language to ask us to help.

I know, concise seems like such a silly word when we have so much to say! Still, when it comes time to ask for help, we do everyone a favor by using direct language.

It worked for this woman, who was frustrated with her dog. She says, "I communicated that I needed my husband's help in the morning to feed the dog and let him out, and the outcome was very positive. I suggested a simple solution, and he said, "I can do that."

And here's the best part, ladies: as you learn how to communicate with your husband about daily tasks, it becomes easier to begin talking about relational issues.

Win/win.

Direct, concise, and specific meets your man's needs, so he can meet yours!

Thoughts: _____

_____

_____

Action Step: _____

_____

July 14

Wives, this week we've been talking about clearly and concisely asking your husband for help. "What was that, honey?"

Rather than tell Jay the trash is full, I now ask him to take it out… right away. Affirmative!

This keeps both of us happier, especially in the kitchen. The truth is, we've found out over the years, that nothing shuts down our communication faster than pride. Instead of simply stating our needs, pride drives a wedge of doubt between you and your spouse by telling you they should know better.

So if you're ready to watch a movie, and your husband sits down in the recliner instead of on the couch next to you, don't waste a minute letting pride stand between you. If you want him next to you, voice your need,

It's not a demand but an opportunity for him to be the one who comes through for you and makes you smile.

Keep asking for what you need in a positive way, and chances are you, your relationship will grow. And your popcorn will be more evenly distributed.

Thoughts: _____
_____
_____
_____

Action Step: _____
_____

July 15

Some of us wear our "busyness" like a badge of honor—until our schedule crowds out everyone, including our spouse!

Ken and Sue experienced the rat race when Ken was offered a great job out of town, and Sue stayed behind to work her own job while taking care of the kids.

Three years into Ken being gone every workweek, husband and wife began to realize something had to change. It became clear: something's gotta give!

When the demands of life and work overtake us, it's time to consider what is most important: not a job, but a life—and a marriage.

To fight for their union, Ken and Sue will have to make a tough choice about whose job to keep, and who needs to look for a new one for the sake of nurturing a family life they can intentionally invest in.

What about you? Does your marriage face a time of tough decision-making? Remember, at the end of the day, there is no relationship on this earth more important than the one you share with your spouse.

Thoughts: _____

_____

_____

_____

Action Step: _____

_____

July 16

When it comes to life—and marriage—it's important that we never stop growing.

Take us, for example. We've been married ___ years, and I still learn something new about Laura every day!

The truth is the minute we stop learning, we stop growing. And that leaves us stagnant in life and bored in our marriages.

So read the newspaper. Invite a friend to join you for lunch. Listen to new music together. Take a class to learn a new language. Or discover a new hobby.

The year we installed a birdfeeder in our backyard, our whole family grew in knowledge. As we fed the birds, we discovered we could influence which ones stopped by for a nibble by the type of feed we put in their tray!

In marriage, our root systems are intertwined, just like two trees. So as we grow up side-by-side, we share nutrients and need feedback from each other to be healthy and whole.

So tackle a new discovery head-on, alone or together—and watch how it helps your marriage grow.

Thoughts: _____
_____
_____
_____

Action Step: _____
_____

JULY 17

I heard a phrase in college that stuck: "If you were both the same, one of you wouldn't be necessary."

And it's not just fun and games… Because if you both had the same emotions, the same way of thinking, and the same social makeup, one of you would be redundant.

So… "How do we grow to appreciate each other's differences?"

Here's how some folks are building emotional intimacy in their marriages:

"When I'm upset, I call my behavior 'processing'; she calls it sulking. Eventually, the dark cloud goes away and I open up more and more to share with my wife how I have been feeling…."

"When I have had a terrible day with our son, when it gets to me, he knows that all I need is some support, even when all I can do is cry."

Different emotional needs, and different opportunities for spouses to make room for each other. On the road to becoming one in marriage, understanding the responses of your spouse will take time, humor, and intention. And it will be worth it!

Thoughts: _____
_____
_____
_____

Action Step: _____
_____

July 18

You may already know that you and your spouse have different emotional needs…

That's for sure!

But did you know that taking the time to understand your spouse's current emotional filter can bond you for life?

One man who experienced the emotional filter of anger explained how his marriage helped this way:

"My father, a preacher for more than twenty years, left my mom for another woman. No one seemed to understand me but my wife. It was as if she felt every pain I felt. I love her for that."

Where does it start? It starts with empathy, or entering into the feeling of your spouse's emotions.

And remember, this isn't about expressing emotions in the same way as your spouse. You're different. Instead, it's about identifying the emotional filter that is occurring in your spouse at a particular time—what is he or she experiencing? Then you choose to feel the pain, anger, loss, or guilt along with him or her. This is where emotional intimacy in your marriage begins.

Thoughts: _____
_____
_____

Action Step: _____
_____

July 19

Sometimes your spouse voices an irrational fear . . .

[Jay coughs]

Jay, it's time to call the doctor!

Instead of using your "annoyed" reflex, it might be wise to consider that your spouse is using an emotional filter.

The summer before I met Jay, my dad passed away. While it has been 30 years since then, I still get very worried when anything goes wrong with Jay's health, even it if just a cough! The truth is, my emotional filter at these times is loss and the fear of losing my spouse like my mom did.

Every spouse will eventually use the emotional filter of loss. John lost two friends and a grandparent in one year—and he began seeing life through an emotional filter of pain and loss. Gratefully, his wife Jane recognized this and allowed him to experience his emotions. When it dribbled over into other situations, like overreacting with their kids, Jane made room.

So consider the emotional filters you are using in your marriage, and discover the benefits of making room for them.

Thoughts: _____
_____
_____
_____

Action Step: _____
_____

July 20

Feeling guilty?

Early in their marriage, Sally and her husband moved back to the state where she had grown up. Sally began to feel guilty because her former boyfriend, with whom she had an intimate relationship in the past, was on her mind.

Guilt from the past can be for things done or not done. The emotional filter of guilt can destroy a relationship if the husband and wife are not open and honest about the situation. Sally may not have believed she was worthy of the love of her husband. And a man who feels guilty for perusing an inappropriate magazine may not feel worthy of his wife's affection.

Sally's breakthrough came when she shared her feelings with her husband, and he assured her it was normal. "Because of his forgiveness and acceptance," Sally said, "I never thought about it again."

If you're carrying guilt in your marriage—or you suspect your spouse is—opening up communication and offering love and forgiveness can be the first step toward wholeness.

Thoughts: _____

_____

_____

Action Step: _____

_____

July 21

Sometimes we're unaware of the emotional filter our spouse might be wearing . . .

But often, we can figure it out by carefully connecting the dots in life. The truth is, each person's filter is different and can change repeatedly with life's circumstances.

For instance, years ago, my mom had cancer and was only given six weeks to live. But God intervened, and she's still kicking! As you can imagine, Doyce's health created emotional fear and sadness in Jay's family. Now anytime she has an abnormality or needs a procedure, all of the emotion floods back.

After one of her procedures and a good report, my dad offered to buy everyone lunch out of the blue. It was simply an outlet for the emotion and anxiety everyone had been feeling.

Is Jay's dad a Christian? Yes! Does he trust that God is in control? Absolutely.

But that doesn't erase our human emotions. And that's why discovering the emotional filter your spouse is using in a particular situation can be the start of watching the emotional intimacy in your marriage rise.

Thoughts: _____
_____
_____
_____

Action Step: _____
_____

July 22

The letter of the day is "C"... If you're cookie monster it stands for "cookies!"

If you're a married couple... It often stands for "conflict."

Take it from us, working through conflict together is necessary to build a saner and more satisfying marriage.

We had our first fight when we were engaged and attending a conference with Jay's family. At the end of a long day, I was famished and craving some oreo cookies. I offered to go buy them but wasn't about to pay over three dollars for eight cookies!

Exhausted and angry, I thought: what an inconsiderate slob, what a cheapskate...

Somehow, we both agreed to the 100-year principle that day. If it won't matter in 100 years, it doesn't matter now.

And we learned something that day: Jay is tight with the buck and I am spoiled! To this day, conflict is the thing that keeps us learning and growing together.

So tend to the necessary conflict in your marriage. Then you can move on to happier "C" words like caring, creativity ... and cookies.

Thoughts: _____

_____

_____

Action Step: _____

_____

JULY 23

How well are you listening to your spouse? A typical marriage includes typical communication . . . short, unclear messages delivered in the fog of daily activities.

Like the wife who once said she wanted to "hear the pitter-patter of little feet," so her husband came home with...a hamster.

All kidding aside, if your communication is breaking down, you may be missing obvious solutions that are right in front of you. So ask yourself, how many times have I misunderstood my spouse this week?

Initiate daily time in which you look him or her in the eye and listen to what he or she is saying...making sure you understand correctly.

For instance: "What I hear you say is that you want me to pick up your dry cleaning, too...not just my own!"

5-10 minutes of intentional listening and communication with your partner just might bring your scattered world into better focus. The truth is we take time to listen to those who give us important information . . . and your spouse should be #1 on the list.

Thoughts: _____

_____

_____

_____

Action Step: _____

_____

July 24

In a culture caught up in a focus on "Self," it's no wonder most of struggle with selfishness.

We even have a "Self" magazine to help us focus even more on…ourselves.

But as a Christian, we have a different model. We know from Scripture we are infinitely valued and loved by God, as seen in Psalm 139. We love a God who knew everything about us even before we were born!

Yet through the example of God's Son, Jesus, this great God also took on flesh…and then completely emptied himself, like a slave…pouring himself out for us!

The compassion Jesus feels for us is the same compassion he longs for us to offer our spouse.

True compassion feels what another is feeling—and then acts in a way that helps that person handle the situation in front of them.

When we demonstrate this compassion to our spouse, we "lose" ourselves in the graciousness of the act. But in the end, we "win" by creating an atmosphere where true love is shown.

Thoughts: _____

_____

_____

Action Step: _____

_____

July 25

Psychology Today article "It's Not All About You" offers a solution for our harried, anxiety-prone culture... Wonder!

When we shift from negative thinking to consider the beauty and immensity of the world around us, our well-being improves. Those who live in urban areas are more likely to be anxious or depressed, for instance. But the article reports that when they visit nature-rich environments, stress hormones lower immediately.

Psalm 19 reminds us of the awe and wonder we find in gazing at Creation, especially when we ascribe all this beauty to a loving and generous Creator:

The heavens declare the glory of God; the skies proclaim the work of his hands.

Day after day they pour forth speech; night after night they reveal knowledge.

Today, let's slow down long enough to notice how small we are.

And what's good for one is doubly good for two. So how about it? Find an activity that will remind you and your spouse it's not all about you. Then breathe deeply, and enjoy all that wonder.

**April 2016, Psychology Today

Thoughts: _____

_____

_____

_____

Action Step: _____

_____

July 26

Ever heard someone say, "What's your Return on Investment?"

In the business world, a strong ROI convinces people to invest money or commit resources to contracts and projects that will go the distance.

And just like in life, your return on investment in marriage will depend on what you put into it. As one woman jokingly said, "Marriage is mostly work."

We would revise that statement to say that when you put the work in, it allows your marriage to flourish and even delight you with its possibilities and potential.

But many couples often ask: How do we make that happen with our crazy lives?

The answers are simple, but not easy. First, you ruthlessly eliminate obligations that are keeping you from living a sustainable life where your commitments matter. Second, you prioritize communication with your spouse so that you check in with each other often, building understanding, cooperation, and a shared mission.

Simplifying and communicating are two great ways to move toward a greater return on investment in your marriage.

Thoughts: _____
_____
_____
_____

Action Step: _____
_____

JULY 27

This week we are featuring five days of date night ideas that can keep your marriage fires burning.

After couples tie the knot, many say their social intimacy goes down. But there's an easy fix for that: spend time together doing things.

It's actually comical to watch how easy it is to forget what you enjoy doing together when you get into the rhythms of married life. Also known as a "rut."

So here are three doable ideas for your next date night. Feel free to pick one or choose all three!

- There is live music somewhere close. Find it and enjoy an evening of music.
- Take her for ice cream, buy a milkshake, and share the straw.
- And lastly, make his favorite dish and dump the kids at a friends house, and return the favor for your friends later.

Get all 52 of our date night ideas by signing up for our email list at JayandLaura.com.

Thoughts: _____
_____
_____
_____

Action Step: _____
_____

July 28

Hello, Laura? This is Jay. I was just wondering if you'd like to go on a date this Friday night?

Those were the days! If it's been too many moons since your spouse asked you out on a bonafide date, you've come to the right place.

That's why we're here to jumpstart your social intimacy by offering you three more doable date ideas you can use…

The sooner, the better! Feel free to pick one or to choose all three:

- Go out for breakfast Saturday morning, then come home and detail the cars.
- Go to the toy store, but a kite together, and fly it on a windy afternoon.
- It is garage sale season! Whoever finds the silliest garage sale item, picks dinner!

The bottom line is it's important for the two of you to find time to spend together doing things you'll both enjoy. So grab an idea and go with it! You might be surprised at the laughter, fun, and intimacy you find.

Thoughts: _____
_____
_____

Action Step: _____
_____

July 29

Laura and I have easily gone on 1,000 dates together. And we're just getting started!

Over the years we've had date nights that ranged from formal or fun to watching a movie in our pjs. And many of them have ended with an intimacy that kept our marriage grounded during times of stress.

But if the thought of being creative feels overwhelming right now, never fear: Jay and Laura to the rescue, with 3 more doable date night ideas.

- Plan a Saturday drive with just the two of you to your favorite beach. Enjoy the sun or watch the sun set.
- Get dressed up to go to a fancy, but start by ringing the front doorbell and opening her car door.
- After dinner, go for a walk and stay out till dark.

The bottom line is it's important for the two of you to find time to spend together doing things you'll both enjoy. So grab an idea or two and go with it!

Thoughts: _____

_____

_____

_____

Action Step: _____

_____

JULY 30

Hello, Date Night hotline.

You've got to help me! My husband and I are fresh out of date night ideas. In fact, I hate to admit this to a stranger...but we've forgotten how to date!

Oh dear. Well, never fear m'lady, I'm confident you can fix this. Just sit down together, remind yourselves of the brains God gave you in the first place and what it felt like to use them to plan dates before you were married, and voila—

Does the thought of planning a date have you breaking out in a sweat? Never fear: Jay and Laura to the rescue, with 3 more doable date night ideas.

- Go to a local nursery and get flowers to plant, then spend the rest of the day working together in the yard.
- Surprise your spouse with tickets to a major or minor league baseball game.
- Do a progressive date...eat appetizers at one restaurant, entree at another, and finish with dessert at a third.

Thoughts: _____
_____
_____

Action Step: _____
_____

July 31

This just in: an Internet sensation is launching date night into another dimension! Behold, the glory of Pinterest, the winning ways of Instagram, and the date night power found in a single facebook post.

It's date night-in-a-box. And not only can it add variety and sizzle to your marriage—it's a fun and personal gift for another couple who could use a meaningful way to make their one-on-one time together matter.

And the best part is you can easily make your own by typing "date night in a box" in the search on Pinterest and going wild with favorites like date-in-a-box fondue night, date night at home for new parents, explore-a-city date night box, or even placing 52 date night ideas in a jar and surprising yourself every week or two.

Our friends David and Suzanne received a date night box, complete with a restaurant gift card, puzzles and playdoh for use while waiting for food, and questions that got them out of their date-night rut and dreaming about their future. Behold, the power of pinterest!

Thoughts: _____
_____
_____
_____

Action Step: _____
_____

August 1

Gentleman, have you ever considered what your wife smells?

For years now, Jay has been on a mission to get men to shower before bed. It's simply impossible for me to understand how a man can jump into bed with all of the odor of a long day's work and hope for closeness and intimacy with his wife.

Along the way, I've answered every excuse in the book:

> "A shower wakes me up in the morning."
>
> So can drinking water, brushing your teeth, and splashing cold water on your face.
>
> "My skin gets too dry if I shower twice a day."
>
> Simple: It's called lotion.
>
> "I simply prefer my showers in the morning."
>
> Let's get real: it's time to consider a real-life way to communicate "I love you" to your wife.

The truth is a woman's sense of smell is more acute than a man's, and your attention to being clean will often make your wife want to love you back.

Thoughts: _____
_____
_____
_____

Action Step: _____
_____

August 2

Behold, the power of tender touch, through affection and actions, to keep a marriage strong, secure, and intimate!

These survey responses come from men who have learned the power of non-sexual touching in creating happy marriages:

"One day while she was at work I cleaned the house top to bottom. Did all the laundry and had supper on the table when she got home, complete with a rose and a note that said "I miss you."

"This is a daily process that starts with an "I love you" hug and continues throughout the day in conversation of loving her. Communicating how she looks and communicating with touch "without being asked to" with hugs and pats—not groping."

And one woman said, "He tells me all the time. By brushing my shoulder whenever he walks past me, praying with me in the morning, snuggling with me after a hard day, and listening to my struggles with clients."

So give it a try. These tender touches have the power to keep your marriage strong, secure, and intimate.

Thoughts: _____
_____
_____
_____

Action Step: _____
_____

AUGUST 3

Some say a woman marries a man hoping he will change; a man marries a woman hoping she will never change.

But as a woman matures, a variety of physical and emotional changes are ushered in. I've even nicknamed this new season "mental-pause."

The same hormones that provide a woman's monthly cycle can also greatly affect our wives emotionally during these changes. The reality is that words spoken at any moment—by any individual—can cause my sensitivity meter to go up, down, or way off the chart!

A word to the wise. During this highly charged time for women, let's carefully guard our thoughts, like: "I liked her better when she was no screaming."

But seriously, significant non-sexual touches can work wonders during this difficult time. Here's a comment from a wife whose husband has carefully guarded his heart and hers: "My husband makes me feel beautiful on the days I feel the worst. When I am having a hormonal, insecure day, he seems to say the right thing . . . most of the time."

Thoughts: _____

_____

_____

_____

Action Step: _____

_____

August 4

When it comes to sewing, I'm all thumbs! Ouch! But I'm not entirely against the idea…

The Dutch word "naaien" means "to sew together so that it can never be separated."

The concept was important for sailors—because they had to sew their sails together in a tight bond to survive the strong winds and rolling seas of the North Atlantic. The same is also true of marriage.

We must be sewn together in such a way, as one flesh, that we can withstand the strong winds— The sickness, the job loss, the relational challenges— That we inevitably stumble across on the rolling seas of life.

As we have become sewn together, we have lifted our marriage, making it our absolute first priority outside of our relationship with God. We're far from perfect, but as a result, we have grown a union that operates not as "Jay" and "Laura," but as "the marriage of Jay and Laura."

This sewn-together intimacy is possible for you too. Find out more in our book The Spark: Igniting the Passion, Mystery, and Romance in Your Marriage.

Thoughts: _____

_____

_____

_____

Action Step: _____

_____

August 5

When you sign up for marriage, you learn that sharing is caring…

Except when it comes to my toothbrush!

It's not long before you realize there is no one closer than your spouse.

We have found that most men report feeling the most intimacy when they make love to your spouse. No surprise there.

But the same is not true for women. A woman feels closest to her guy when he is in tune with her thoughts, desires, and feelings.

For example, when Jay finishes a sentence for me, and I say, "That is exactly what I was thinking!" Or when he suggests going out for a chef salad at a local café, and I say, "I've been craving that for two days." Or when he senses I'm overwhelmed and asks, "What can I take off your plate?" In those moments, I know there is no one closer than my husband.

Learning how to cherish Laura has made our marriage stronger and two-toothbrush household more satisfying for both of us. How will you cherish your spouse today?

Thoughts: _____
_____
_____
_____

Action Step: _____
_____

August 6

Are you having a great day... Or a horrible one?

Whatever turns up, spouses have made the commitment: I will stand right by your side. Does your husband or wife know you've got his or her back?

Life can be so unpredictable that rock-solid marriages where a spouse stands by their partner stand out. In an 18-month stretch where many of my friends were diagnosed with cancer, I watched their husbands stand by them through radiation, chemotherapy, surgery, and great uncertainty. Instead of bolting, these men honored their commitment to stand right by their spouses.

Another woman wrote about the power of this kind of partnership: "I work full time and my husband has been quite ill for the past three years. He is also a wonderful cook. God has been good... and he is doing well right now...I came home from work, and my husband had fixed a wonderful supper, had flowers on the table, and a beautiful card that simply stated thanks for being by my side."

Consider reminding your husband or wife today: I'll stand by you, no matter what.

Thoughts: _____
_____
_____
_____

Action Step: _____
_____

AUGUST 7

Some days you push more of your spouse's buttons than on other days…

Sometimes you push your spouse's buttons on every day that ends in "Y"!

That's why a facebook user emailed us asking us how to stop:

"When this happens, I get angry and I hurt my husband and then he gets angry and cuts me off…he has a long fuse and I have a short fuse…We both recognize our tendency to do this and are working on it, but we've been married 19 years and it's still an issue."

The truth is, you learn over time what buttons not to push. And you can also make a commitment to talk about it when it does happen, to begin to develop habits that address that short fuse and long fuse, so you address issues early on, ask for forgiveness, and don't allow things to fester.

If you have a short fuse, count to 10 before speaking…

For someone with a long fuse, realize that life is too short to hold a grudge, forgive and move on…and move back toward your biggest fan.

Thoughts: _____

_____

_____

Action Step: _____

_____

August 8

Some husbands and wives see each other almost all day, every day…but most of us have limited time together.

Sometimes for days at a time.

And changing these routines sometimes leads to challenging transitions. Like the husband and wife who are facing retirement. Or the wife who wrote to say her husband used to be a trucker, so she only saw him for 1 ½ days on the weekends. Now the two of them have to adjust to seeing each other on a daily basis, and the struggle can be real.

This happened to Jay and I when he would travel every weekend and the kids and I would have a party until he returned. Often I felt like I missed out on all the fun!

And that's where the conversations have to start. Start by realizing that life is filled with transitions. And say, *this is a new transition for us…here's how this makes me feel. Here are some adjustments we need to make. We can face this transition together…and communication is what will make it work.* You can do this!

Thoughts: _____
_____
_____
_____

Action Step: _____
_____

August 9

Today, our parents answer the question: "What does it take to make it to your 50th wedding anniversary?"

"It takes a lot of energy. And a lot of patience. Be nice to each other."

"The first thing I would say is we have to have two forgivers. In the long run, if you can't forgive each other for the little things you won't forgive each other for the big things."

"Well I would say, it's very important to laugh a lot together. A few years ago, Jay and Laura gave us dancing lessons for a Christmas gift. We had a hard time getting our minds to communicate with our feet . . . It was doggone hilarious!"

And the final words of wisdom coming from my mom as she glanced at my dad: "Brush your teeth!"

We encourage *you* to seek out committed couples who have been married for a long time and ask them what their secret is. All of us could benefit from a little golden anniversary wisdom!

Thoughts: _____
_____
_____
_____

Action Step: _____
_____

August 10

Time to connect a significant obstacle in your marriage relationship? Join the club! For many couples, especially when both spouses have demanding jobs, nurturing their love takes heroic efforts.

Here's a list of things to consider when addressing balance:

- Make a family mission statement, and ask yourself, Is having that second job part of who you want to be as a couple?
- With two incomes, consider hiring someone to clean house and mow lawn, creating more time for the two of you.
- Make a family calendar for the month. Put any kids' activities or other commitments on there. Then schedule a date night in red, even if it conflicts with something else your kids are doing. Your date night must be sacred.

Finally, although the world around you may elevate efficiency as the #1 virtue, remember that an efficient marriage isn't necessarily an effective one. God has given you your marriage as a precious resource to be guarded, nurtured, and protected. Make your work-home balance work for your marriage.

Thoughts: _____
_____
_____
_____

Action Step: _____
_____

August 11

What happens when she's in the mood—but he's not?

Today, many women are asking us this question: how often does a wife have more desire for intimacy than her husband? Speaking frankly, studies show this happens in 20% of marriages—1 out of 5 marriages. And many women out there experiencing this are just as frustrated as the men who experience it in reverse.

That's why we're speaking out today to assure you this is perfectly normal, and that you're not alone. More and more women are bringing this struggle out into the open.

The bottom line is this: you've got to communicate. Let your husband know how you feel, and that this is a great need for you. And husbands, if this applies to your marriage, it would be helpful for you to acknowledge the reality of your situation to your wife. Let her know you do love her, you do find her attractive, but you have physical differences. Communication is always the first step in meeting each other's needs.

Thoughts: _____
_____
_____

Action Step: _____
_____

August 12

It's a common question: What do I do with the unintentional hurt my spouse is causing me?

Not long ago, a man emailed us:

"I love my wife and greatly appreciate all that she does. She is raising our 4 kids with one more on the way. Sometimes, though, she does things that really hurt me. She doesn't intend to hurt me [so]I don't talk to her about these things."

No matter what stress your wife is under, she's unaware, and she deserves to know so she can fix what she's doing.

Here's a great way to start the conversation: When she does something that hurts you, say **help me understand**, why you did that? Then follow up with, "Did you understand that when you did that you hurt me?"

Or try: "Did you realize you hurt me when you did _____."

Both approaches are a great communication-starter, especially when you also express appreciation. Our advice: don't ever let continual hurt feelings fester: it's best for both of you if you address them.

Thoughts: _____

_____

_____

_____

Action Step: _____

_____

August 13

Experiencing midlife crisis? We can relate.

Recently, a facebook fan named this as their greatest challenge in marriage. As we age, we've tried to stop counting the things that are over, and start saying, this is the beginning of…

Some new opportunity, ministry, or recreational event we can explore.

But first, it might be wise to develop the power to laugh at the changes that are here and still coming…whether you're ready or not. Where Laura used to dress in 3 layers of clothing and I wore shorts and tshirts in the winter, our body temperatures have suddenly flip-flopped, as well as our wardrobe choices.

This isn't an end, it's a new beginning…and changes will happen. Time to put on your big girl pants and big boy pants and lean into it.

Tonight, sit down and have a conversation about how these midlife changes challenge you. Then make a decision to list the ways in which the glass is still half-full, and chart out the life together that awaits you.

Thoughts: _____
_____
_____
_____

Action Step: _____
_____

August 14

Do you and your spouse sleep in separate bedrooms?

You're not alone. A recent article reports this is a new trend. It even insisted that separate bedrooms could create a spark in a couple's intimate life. As couples are getting married later in life, they've already established some habits, and those can be hard to break.

Here's our take: we believe part of marriage is getting used to those habits, and enjoying the intimacy and closeness that comes from sleeping in the same bed. It can spark conversation, cuddling, or even prayer before you fall to sleep.

So as much as possible, work on good hygiene so you're a good bed partner. Address snoring issues. Use earplugs or communicate to do the best you can to sleep in the same space. And if health issues prevent you from sharing a bed, work all the harder to spend time cuddling, sharing skin-on-skin contact and quiet conversation (among other things) during non-sleeping hours.

Your marriage will benefit from your efforts to cultivate mutual intimacy.

Thoughts: _____
_____
_____
_____

Action Step: _____
_____

August 15

How long has it been since you and your spouse shared a belly laugh?

It's about time, don't you think? After all, laughter can change my perspective, it can change my heart, and it even changes my body chemistry.

No wonder Solomon said in Proverbs 4:23: "Above all else, guard your heart, for it is the wellspring of life."

Laughter is a lubricant that reduces tension and brings the fun back to couples and families.

So consider sharing funny emails, enjoying a funny movie or TV show, or even finding a card or object that will make your spouse giggle.

There will be times when you and your spouse need to set aside time to discuss serious challenges in your marriage. But there should also be times, and plenty of them, when the cares of the world fall away, and you learn to laugh off minor annoyances and habits that aren't to your liking. Try it today, and let us know what happens by emailing us at info@jayandlaura.com.

Thoughts: _____
_____
_____
_____

Action Step: _____
_____

August 16

Is there a universal truth that applies to every man?

Yes! No matter who your man is, he needs to hear: "I want you!"

Before you turn the page, let's talk straight. The truth we've discovered in talking to hundreds of men is that men find a woman's body desirable. No surprise, there.

What women don't always realize is that as a man experiences a desire to be intimate every 72 hours—he longs to share that energy and love with you!

Research shows that in 80% of marriages, the husband has a higher desire for physical intimacy. But even when there's no time for physical intimacy or affection…

When a man knows that his wife wants him, it puts his heart at peace and his world in order.

So remember men have their own kind of cycle about every 72 hours. For the sake of your man and your marriage, paying attention to the way his mind and body work—and letting him know you want him—can lead to a stronger, more satisfying marriage for both of you.

Thoughts: _____
_____
_____
_____

Action Step: _____
_____

August 17

Someone asked Laura: "What is the one thing about Jay that irritates you?"

The funny thing is the thing that irritates me the most is what he's doing right now; Jay has the habit of laughing in the middle of a serious conversation.

I can neither confirm nor deny this accusation!

But truthfully, it can be my defense mechanism when I get in an argument with Laura, in times when I don't want it to go deeper. But that doesn't change the fact that a sense of humor transforms challenges—and by a sense of humor, I mean you have the ability to laugh at yourself. Not your spouse, but yourself! Freedom often comes when you refuse to take yourself so seriously.

The truth is, all of us have something funny about us. It's part of our God-given uniqueness. Rather than hiding it, consider celebrating it. We believe you'll find that by lightening up and laughing at yourself, it can provide relief and joy to your marriage and your family.

Thoughts: _____
_____
_____

Action Step: _____
_____

AUGUST 18

Slip 'n slides, ice cream, and kids home 24/7! There's nothing like the dog days of summer.

Parents, if you're feeling the heat of long summer days...

Take it from two parents whose kids are grown now: embrace every moment you can with slurpee runs and spontaneous fun—but if married, make sure your kids see your marriage is your #1 relationship on this earth.

When frustrations mount this summer, remember the words of James 4, life is short, here today, and gone tomorrow.

Next, remember that kids see how you behave in the tough times, and they will learn from observing your behavior. When times get irritating, use it as teaching moment with your kids. Let them know that mommy or daddy or both are a little frustrated and explain why.

Finally, focus on your marriage. The best thing you can do for your children is to be madly in love with your spouse. Study after study shows that the healthiest, highest achieving, socially connected kids come from a family where mom and dad intentionally work on growing their love.

Thoughts: _____
_____
_____
_____

Action Step: _____
_____

August 19

When was the last time you and your spouse got away?

Please tell me it's not your honeymoon!

Truthfully, we recommend couples make a plan to get away at least two times a year. Once to "play" together doing something fun, and once to work on your marriage together at a seminar or retreat, where you'll get the tools to keep your marriage strong.

Your investment in your marriage up front will shore it up against the hassles of daily life and the stress of unexpected events.

Believe me, over the years we've heard all the excuses: it's too expensive, what do we do with the kids, we like to do different things. These excuses are obstacles easily overcome when you understand the enormous benefits that getting away brings to your relationship.

Reconnecting while away just might rekindle the love 8-year-old Emily referred to: "Love is when you kiss all the time, then when you get tired of kissing you still want to be together and you talk more. Mommy and daddy are like that. They look gross when they kiss."

Thoughts: _____

_____

_____

Action Step: _____

_____

August 20

I'll let you in on a secret: Most men want nothing more than to make their wife happy.

As the comedian Jeff Allen says: happy wife, happy life. Because when our wife is smiling or laughing, we know she's happy.

And that laughter produces a physical change: ladies, when you laugh, endorphins release, and the effect is like a natural opiate or drug.

Just as Proverbs 7:22 says, A joyful heart is good medicine, a study at a hospital showed that when they got patients laughing, they healed quicker.

It's also a key ingredient in a healthy marriage. That's why we like to make people laugh. Because we know laughter lasts beyond the moment. When your guard goes down, and you begin to laugh together, your intimacy and togetherness goes up.

So find a joke of the day, or go to a website like MikeysFunnies.com to subscribe to clean humor that can make everything lighter and brighter. That's your prescription: from laugh doctors, Jay and Laura Laffoon.

Thoughts: _____
_____
_____
_____

Action Step: _____
_____

August 21

Martin Luther once said, "I judge the depth of a man's faith by his ability to laugh."

But the truth is, even though we inject laughter into marriages, sometimes we can be sourpusses ourselves.

Recently, we were in Anaheim, CA, doing a show, when we stopped by Starbucks for our favorite drinks. I went to order as Jay said: Trente shaken black tea, no classic, no water.

So Laura told the barista she needed two Trente shaken black teas, no classic, no water. "Does that mean no ice?" the barista said. "Sure," I said.

Except that Jay decided tea without ice isn't really "iced tea." And he brought it back for ice, feeling a little hot and bothered!

Just the night before we had taught, "Is what we're facing going to matter in a hundred years??" It was at that moment that Laura asked me the same, instigating holy laughter.

Does iced tea really need ice? Or is ice a form of water? You decide. But either way, make sure you laugh together today.

Thoughts: _____
_____
_____
_____

Action Step: _____
_____

August 22

Here's a common question: What should I do if my spouse won't go to church with me?

We believe Church is important, but we've also realized there are many reasons spouses don't want to go to church. They may not share your faith, or they may have issues with their faith. That's why this is a question that should be worked out before marriage.

After marriage, it takes work and compromise to figure out. If both of you love each other, communicating your feelings openly and talking things through is a first step. Sometimes counseling can help, whether you go alone or your spouse agrees to come along, too.

But remember this: just because it's a beautiful thing for spouses to worship together, it doesn't mean you have to skip church if your spouse does. Find a church community where you can worship, learn, be in community, and serve. The health of your relationship with Christ can greatly impact your marriage. So if your spouse won't go to church with you, control what you can control: yourself.

Thoughts: _____
_____
_____
_____

Action Step: _____
_____

August 23

What is the most important kind of communication a couple needs in a marriage? Could it be...

- Communication about finances?
- Communication about family or the future?
- Conflict resolution communication? (oh boy!)
- Or how about intimate or playful communication? (now that sounds like fun!)

Though there are endless things couples should be communicating about, the truth is the most important communication you need is your communication with Jesus. As we grow closer to him, we naturally grow closer to our spouse. Maybe that's doing daily devotions, going on a prayer walk, or praying together.

For Laura and I, we appreciate different kinds of devotionals, so we each take time to read a short one each morning. Later in the day, we sit down face to face to share what we learned. Double the blessing.

When you focus on the Lord, you take your eyes off yourself, and you begin to see the needs of others, including your spouse. That's why the most important communication you can engage in today is the kind that draws you closer to Christ.

Thoughts: _____
_____
_____

Action Step: _____
_____

August 24

Here's our question: When was the last time you laid down your life for your spouse?

John 15:13 says, "Greater love has no one than this, that he laid down his life for his friend."

This is about putting aside your own agenda. It's not necessarily a big thing—but it's putting your wife first in the small things every day. Several years ago, I started making the bed for us, after 20 years of Laura doing it.

I think for most women, they would be so grateful just to have their spouse sit down across from them and intently listen. And as wives think of how to serve their husbands, we believe it's important for women to remember to put their husband's needs above their children's needs. This requires planning and intention.

Offering yourself to each other is a continual process, as you constantly look to care for and lay down your life for your spouse. As you walk with God, he reveals new ways each of you can serve that will bless both you and your marriage for years to come.

Thoughts: _____
_____
_____

Action Step: _____
_____

August 25

Is character more important than competence in marriage? Or is it the other way around?

Actually, it's both. Author Stephen Covey writes: "Character is who we are; competence is what we can do. Both are necessary."

So what does character in marriage mean? It means what is often a countercultural act of remaining faithful and staying committed to your vows and your spouse.

What does competence mean? HOW are you being faithful? How are you doing at the work of marriage?

Truthfully, it takes courage to not be transformed to this world. "Courage is not the absence of fear; courage is fear turned inside out."

We all have moments of incompetence; but courage helps us to stick with what you said you're going to do. Character means staying true; competence means making habits that will grow your character and your marriage. And trust us, when you grow your marriage, you grow yourself; both you and your marriage will benefit from a commitment to character and competence.

Thoughts: _____
_____
_____

Action Step: _____
_____

August 26

What should our response be when we watch our spouse fail?

I fail often with my tone of voice. And I can unintentionally hurt Laura deeply. That's when she says, "Do you know you just made me feel absolutely stupid?"

Earlier in our marriage, I messed up our finances, and we found ourselves swimming in $2,000 of credit card debt.

Both of us have failed countless times in marriage. And we've learned how our families of origin dealt with conflict is going to surface with our spouse. I can be a bulldozer or an avoider—and I want to see it addressed fairly and resolved.

Because you're human, you will fail. Quite possibly, you may let your spouse down more than anyone else on this planet. But failure isn't final.

When I messed up our finances, I saw it as an opportunity to learn. 20-something years later, I understand budget, and I'm managing our money well.

The moral of the story is this: when our spouse fails, we pick them up, help them learn, and help them grow.

Thoughts: _____
_____
_____
_____

Action Step: _____
_____

August 27

How does your spouse measure up to the example of your opposite sex parent?

My mom is an amazing cook who baked delicious bread every Saturday morning!

After getting married, I immediately started comparing Laura's cooking to my mom's. In fact, I unfairly compared them in many ways, trying to change Laura. One day I "gently" reminded Jay that he was not married to his mother!

Women already compare themselves to other women. Am I as pretty as she is? As smart? Am I as good of a mother as my friend is? That's why when a woman's husband compares her to other women, he does serious damage to her and to their marriage.

Know this: the spouse God gave us is all we will ever need in our marriage. When you grasp the idea that your spouse, given to you by God, is all you ever need, you start looking at that person in an entirely different light. Look for the good and not the bad, the helpful not the hurtful, and your marriage will grow strong.

Thoughts: _____

_____

_____

Action Step: _____

_____

August 28

What does it mean to "woo" her… And to "wow" him?

Take a minute and think of the many ways you wooed or wowed your spouse while dating. Have you done anything remotely like that recently?

Remember noticing what pleased them? And surprising them with your love? Here are just a few ways to reconnect:

- pull out your phone at lunch and text your spouse with a loving message
- leave notes around the house
- plan a romantic interlude or a special meal or trip to rekindle the spark in your marriage.

We were at one of our date night events when we witnessed a couple in their 80s, holding hands, obviously happy to be in love. When we talked to the man, he said: You tell them that "What you did to get her is what you gotta do to keep her."

This week, why not take the flame on the backburner in your marriage and bring it to the front, then turn up the heat. Woo her—and wow him.

Thoughts: _____
_____
_____
_____

Action Step: _____
_____

August 29

When was the last time you and your spouse got away?

If you can't remember, it's time for a crash course in the benefits of getting away so you can get ahead in your marriage.

As you consider a possible fall getaway, here are 4 great reasons to make it a top priority:

REST – Break out of your daily routine to create new opportunities of communication, fun, and intimacy with your spouse.

RECREATION – Even if you can only plan "a day away," chances are you and your spouse can find several fun things to do together in succession—maybe you'll even be wildly spontaneous!

REJUVENATION – The word means to "make young again," bringing life back to your marriage. Science tells us that feelings of being "in love" begin to fade after about 18 months unless we purposefully act to keep the spark alive.

RECONNECTION – This is when we remember why we feel in love in the first place.

So grab your spouse, a calendar, and a pen. It's time to plan a getaway that is uniquely you!

Thoughts: _____
_____
_____
_____

Action Step: _____
_____

August 30

When Laura walked down our wedding aisle, marriage seemed magical. Maybe it was all the romantic movies that portray couples always waking up in each other's arms! Never mind the reality of sweaty sheets or bad breath!

Ask a couple married any length of time, and they know the reality of marriages ups and downs. As the days go on, it's vital that you change your thinking about what marriage is and what it means to both of you.

There's a time when you need to be reminded that God has a plan for the two of you to use you for a good purpose in His Kingdom.

We've found that the ways to do this include drawing close to the Lord yourself, so you can operate on a full emotional, spiritual, and relational tank, rather than an empty one.

Spend time with another couple who love marriage and are having fun together.

And find a common mission—that thing you are both passionate about that can help you transform your time, love, and priorities—together.

Thoughts: _____
_____
_____
_____

Action Step: _____
_____

August 31

We've all done it. Who doesn't like to avoid conflict?

"I said I'm fine!"

So I offer the silent treatment for a day or two, or I storm out of the room, and nothing productive happens in our marriage.

There's a better way to argue, and we're here to teach you how:

First, realize it's normal for two people from two different backgrounds to have conflict. You're not alone!

Second, know that family issues, money, and intimacy will be hot-button triggers for conflict. Sometimes you can see an argument coming, and prepare a better way to deal with it.

And third, you should actually get worried when you stop arguing. In fact, the habitual avoidance of conflict is the number one predictor of divorce.

What's sad is the reason couples avoid conflict is because they believe it causes divorce. Successful couples learn how to manage their areas of disagreement and live life "around" them – to keep talking and arguing and loving in spite of their differences and to develop understanding and empathy for their partner's positions.

Thoughts: _____
_____
_____
_____

Action Step: _____
_____

September 1

Can arguing be a sign of a healthy marriage? Ever heard of the couple who explain to their marriage counselor, "We never talk anymore. We figured out that's when we do all our fighting."

At first, we avoid conflict because we are in love and we believe that "staying in love" is about agreeing and NOT fighting. We're afraid we'll run our marriage into the ditch. And that we should just agree about the most important things.

While it's true that we don't get married to handle conflict, if a couple doesn't learn how to manage their disagreements successfully, their marriage won't thrive. We see couples who are so determined to avoid disagreements that they shut down – quit talking, quit loving.

Couples need to know what the research has found: that every happy, successful couple has approximately ten areas of "incompatibility" or disagreement that they will never resolve. Wow.

Successful couples learn how to manage their areas of disagreement and live life "around" them – loving in spite of their differences and developing empathy and appreciation for their partner's differences.

Thoughts: _____
_____
_____
_____

Action Step: _____
_____

September 2

You know things are tense when neighbors can no longer talk to each other without pushing someone's political or personal buttons.

We can't change the way the world is…but we do have a choice in how we respond. Inside marriage, we've found 4 ways to fortify our lives represented by the word "FORT."

F – FAITH Scripture tells us to love our neighbor, and if you're married, your closest neighbor happens is your spouse. Lift them up; love them; protect and honor them.

O- OBSESSION Our country is obsessed by the latest gossip, political scandal, or item they can acquire. But Philippians 4:8 tells us to focus on things that are true, lovely, and of good report.

R – REST The world tells us to keep going 24/7, but God instructs us to rest for a 24-hour period each week, following his example. He's got everything under control.

And finally, T – TRUST Trust holds all relationships together, but especially marriage. Wake up each morning ready to say "I do" and your relationship will go the distance, serving as a protective fortress in uncertain times.

Thoughts: _____
_____
_____
_____

Action Step: _____
_____

September 3

Here is a question we received via email:

"My wife & daughter say it is impersonal to always call your significant other by a nickname, like 'dear,' not by their given name. Would you agree?"

I don't think I would agree that it is impersonal. In the right context it can be very endearing. We had silly nicknames for each other when we first met and got engaged...not gonna share here!

Since then we have let those drop and we rarely use some endearing term for each other....maybe we are just not that endearing! However, we don't think it is wrong. But if your wife doesn't like the nickname and or would prefer you to use her given name, then I would follow her desires!

I think for some couples it is just natural to have a nickname for their spouse and others just don't. Neither is right or wrong..... but always listen to your spouse and what they want!

Thoughts: _____
_____
_____
_____

Action Step: _____
_____

September 4

The continual question...

From a radio listener:

"My greatest challenge in my marriage is submitting to a husband who won't lead!"

I want to be very careful and make sure you hear exactly what I am saying. Ephesians 5:22 says, "wives submit to your husband as you would to the Lord." 1 Peter 3:1 says, "Wives, in the same way submit yourselves to your own husbands so that, if any of them do not believe the word, they may be won over without words by the behavior of their wives"

So, as I read these two passages of scripture, I see two scenarios-- first, submit to your husband in spite of the fact he may not lead, and in that way, you are submitting to the Lord.

Secondly, if your husband is not a believer, you still submit in hopes that your behavior will cause him to believe. The bottom line as I see it is, as wives we submit because we love Jesus!

Thoughts: _____
_____
_____
_____

Action Step: _____
_____

September 5

A listener asks:

"We fight constantly and don't involve God into our marriage. So the greatest challenge in our relationship is to try to build our marriage back up when I feel like it is broken."

Fighting, disagreeing, heated discussions are not bad for your marriage! In fact, the greatest indicator of divorce is the "habitual avoidance of conflict." It is good and healthy for your marriage to argue, as long as it is fair.

When a married couple disagrees, it shows that they care enough about the marriage and each other to voice their opinions. When we reach the point of avoiding conflict, we no longer care.

The other side of this question is more important--involve God in your marriage. As you each grow closer to Him you will grow closer to each other. Pray with and for each other. Having God in your marriage will not make you stop arguing but it will keep you on this journey called marriage.

Thoughts: _____
_____
_____
_____

Action Step: _____
_____

September 6

This Facebook Follower writes;

"The greatest challenge in my relationship with my wife is being honest with her. I want her to like me and I'm afraid of how she will respond to all of my failures. Even after repenting on several occasions and being honest many times with her it is still very hard because I love her and I know that my failures hurt her and I don't want to hurt her."

First understand, we all fail. God gave us our spouse to be helpmates for each other; Ecc 4:9-10 says, "Two are better than one, because they have a good return for their labor: If either of them falls down, one can help the other up." Allowing your wife to see your failures and help you through them will not only strengthen your marriage but will challenge you both to grow spiritually.

The only failure that is permanent is a failure from which you don't get up.

Thoughts: _____
_____
_____

Action Step: _____
_____

September 7

We had a listener ask this question:

"How do you tell your husband what you need without feeling that you're being selfish?"

Ladies, I know how you feel, but here is something I know--your husband only wants to make you happy! He will do anything to make that happen. Your husband's desire to make you happy therefore when you tell them what you need from them--whether it's cleaning up the dishes to putting kids to bed to rubbing your feet--they want to hear it. It is isn't being selfish it is being honest.

I also know two things--men are not mind readers and they don't get subtle hints. We have to be clear with what we need from our husband. Once we spell it out--they will do everything in their power to make it happen!

It might have something to do with what our good friend Jeff Allen says, "happy wife happy life!"

Thoughts: _____
_____
_____
_____

Action Step: _____
_____

September 8

"When my husband doesn't think my viewpoint is correct during a discussion, he cuts me off and starts yelling and pounding his hand on a chair arm. I have told him that it's not respectful and I won't continue the conversation unless he stops yelling. Usually he won't stop yelling, so I don't respond and it ends without resolution. Is there anything else that I can do to get him to not yell and to let me express my thoughts?"

First of all, you are correct in telling him that yelling is disrespectful. Also done well is your refusal to escalate the argument. Find a time when he's in a good mood and ask him this question: "Do you know how it makes me feel when you yell and pound your chair?" Most likely he will say no. Then you can say, "would you like to know?" And hopefully this exercise will open the door for healthy discussion and a resolution to your problem.

Thoughts: _____
_____
_____
_____

Action Step: _____
_____

September 9

Some people are planners and others just aren't. We are planners. We discuss a plan for each day, each week, each month. We plan vacations way ahead!

This listener has a husband who isn't a planner, and she is!

"It is difficult for my husband to plan anything even though he is retired, and sometimes I wonder what he does during the day. We've been empty nesters for two years now, and it is difficult to reconnect and find things to do."

I would say it is perfectly okay for this wife to plan things for them to do as a couple. I would recommend, though, that as a couple they discuss what kinds of activities they would both enjoy. Jay looks ahead to vacations. He loves to look through all the vacation websites and get ideas and information. Then we simply discuss what he has found and we go from there!

Thoughts: _____
_____
_____

Action Step: _____
_____

September 10

Question from a listener:

"My husband travels for a living. When he is gone, we seem to have a good relationship, we talk or skype everyday. When he comes home for long periods of time, we don't get along at all."

We experienced this when he first started traveling and speaking. Life was good when he was on the road--he was living his dream and the rest of us at home kind of did our own thing!

It sounds like heaven but it isn't!

It was an adjustment every time he came home to fit back into the home routine. It took a lot of hard work, deep discussions, and compromise to get our routine down.

Here are a few tips:

- Discuss what is fair to you both when he (or she) is gone.
- Discuss when you are both home, what you want it to look like.
- Commit to it and make it happen.

Thoughts: _____

_____

_____

Action Step: _____

_____

September 11

"Time is our biggest struggle. Finding time for each other while juggling a full time job three kids from high school, elementary, and one in diapers, we feel we never have enough time for each other. And at times it is very stressful on our relationship."

This unfortunately is a very common problem in today's culture. If this is your issue, we need to look at one of two solutions. You may need to improve your time management skills; or, you need to look at your priorities.

If it is a time management issue, know that there are a great number of books or online programs that can help you squeeze every minute out of every day!

If it is a priority issue then something has to give. You and your spouse need to take a look at everything you do and decide what "good" thing you are going to have to give up for the sake of your marriage.

Thoughts: _____
_____
_____
_____

Action Step: _____
_____

September 12

You know those people--the world seems to revolve around them; they are oblivious to others. The real problem comes when it is your spouse:

"Could you give me some advice on how to deal with a husband who is self centered and doesn't know how to control his mouth. He is very arrogant and just says whatever he wants. We've been married for 24 years and I am getting weary of dealing with this."

In this situation there are a few important things to remember:

- My response is my responsibility--responding to a spouse like this with grace and few words is better than reacting every time they blurt out and overreact.

- Picking the right time--look for opportunities to point out the behavior during times that are calm and without tension.

- Prayer is your best weapon for change--praying for your spouse, praying for opportunities for words, praying for others who will speak the truth to them.

Thoughts: _____
_____
_____

Action Step: _____
_____

September 13

"I believe spouses should sleep in one bed together. This has worked really swell for over three years until...my husband's snoring has amplified to the point I get no sleep. We have resorted to sleeping in separate beds. We try to at least lay down a bit together before splitting up to allow for pillow talk time but it's just not the same."

We agree! Spouses should sleep together but snoring is a huge issue for many couples. First we'd recommend a sleep study, because snoring can be a sign of a more significant health issue.

We had this same issue in our marriage (we both snored) but the answer was simple. We cut wheat and dairy out of our diet and the snoring went away. I know that sounds weird, but it was true! Many people have gluten and or lactose issues which can lead to snoring. Say goodbye to bread and milk and hello to a good night's sleep.

Thoughts: _____
_____
_____
_____

Action Step: _____
_____

September 14

"Would you like a gift receipt with that purchase?"

This seems to be a common question when you buy something these days. When giving a gift we almost always ask for a gift receipt in case the recipient doesn't like what we got them. If it isn't the perfect gift or exactly what we wanted, we take it back and exchange it for the precise item we want.

Unfortunately, that mentality has oozed into our thoughts about marriage. If this one isn't the marriage of my dreams, then I'll take this one back and look for an "upgrade".

Marriages don't come with a gift receipt. We believe they should come with a lifetime guarantee! When we stand at the altar, we say to our spouse that we will commit to making this marriage be the best it can possibly be...period.

We honor our spouse, ourselves, but more importantly the Lord when we take "till death do us part" seriously.

Thoughts: _____
_____
_____

Action Step: _____
_____

September 15

We see this more and more in our culture today.

"We are a young couple, starting careers, and really don't want to get married right away. We would like to be 'set' before we do...is it okay for us to live together for a few years?"

The short answer is, no.

If you are committed to each other and to the relationship, then get married. The reality is, you will never have "enough money" to get married. You will never be "ready" to have kids. You will never be "set."

This may sound harsh, but it sounds more like a cop out to getting married. If you are feeling this way, you have to ask yourself, "do I really love this person enough to spend the rest of my life with them?"

If your answer to the question is yes, then make the commitment and get married. If your answer is no, then do the right thing and move on.

A trial run at marriage is never a good thing.

Thoughts: _____
_____
_____
_____

Action Step: _____
_____

September 16

"Four Ways We Are Killing Our Marriage," was the title of the article I read on Relevant Magazine. The first way we are killing our marriage is that as married couples we embrace the bare minimum.

What is the minimum we can do for our marriage. Let's read a book--we get through one chapter and quit reading. Let's go to a seminar--we go to a one day workshop rather than investing in a 8 week-long marriage class. Let's get counseling--we go once and decide it isn't for us.

We look for the easy way to revive our marriage rather than saying we are going to the hard work no matter how long it takes!

Decide as a couple that you are not going to settle for the minimum but you are going to make your marriage the best it can be by investing your time, your labor and your love.

Thoughts: _____
_____
_____

Action Step: _____
_____

September 17

We require everything microwaved, instantaneous, and delivered overnight. If there was an Amazon.com for relationships, we would download it, because we don't want to wait for anything.

There is a business axiom which states, "fast, cheap, or good... pick two." So, to get something fast and cheap means you sacrifice good. This may work in the fast food industry or when it comes to marketing clothing for teens, but not in marriage.

Because marriage is meant for a lifetime we must understand that great marriages are built slowly, expensively, and with great care.

We build our marriage slowly because we want to build it on good foundational habits like quality communication and understanding.

We build our marriage expensively because making our marriage a priority requires a significant investment of our money and time.

We build our marriage with great care because we love our spouse and genuine love lasts a lifetime.

Thoughts: _____
_____
_____

Action Step: _____
_____

September 18

Another way we are killing our marriages according to Relevant Magazine is this:

"We prefer distraction over conversation. When there is potential for a meaningful exchange, we steer it in the other direction because we don't want to risk vulnerability."

After a recent argument between Jay and I that started small enough but ended with me coming at him with of all the things he had said that had hurt me or bothered me over the last several few weeks, I realized I store all these feelings down deep and then let them out all at once--not fair!

A healthy marriage is one where both spouses speak of their feelings rather than push them down.

Thoughts: _____
_____
_____
_____

Action Step: _____
_____

September 19

The last way we are killing our marriage according to Relevant:

"Admitting marital problems, which is even more terrifying if we ourselves are children of divorced parents. There is also the dread of ruining our kids' lives with the truth that "mommy and daddy are having problems." So we plod along, raising children, vacationing and running successful businesses in what appears to be an amazing life."

It's true! We travel all across the country with our Ultimate Date Night show and hear all the time, "We invited Greg and Mary, but they said their marriage is fine," or "When we tell people we are coming to a marriage thing they automatically ask what's wrong with our marriage."

Working on and investing in your marriage, whether it be through books, counseling, education, or simply dating each other, is the best way you can revive your marriage and fall in love again.

Admitting you need help, doing the hard work, is the best thing for you and your spouse and your family!

Thoughts: _____
_____
_____
_____

Action Step: _____
_____

September 20

Did you know, laughter changes your chemistry?

Most people understand that our bodies are little chemical factories. Every day, hundreds of different chemicals course through our bloodstream.

The natural chemicals in our bodies have a great amount of power. Scientists tell us that a variety of emotions can release different chemicals into our bloodstream.

It is widely accepted that one of the reasons people train for endurance athletic events like running and biking is to experience the endorphin rush that follows the event or the training.

These same endorphins are released when a person laughs. Understand, we are not talking about a mere chuckle or a snicker. We mean a laugh, an all-out, make-your-belly-shake-laugh. It doesn't have to be long, but it does need to be a laugh.

Like a powerful drug, endorphins soothe and comfort. Some say they even promote healing. Think about that. When you laugh, you could actually be helping your body heal itself.

Here is to a good belly laugh!

Thoughts: _____
_____
_____
_____

Action Step: _____
_____

September 21

Did you know, laughter changes your attitude?

It has been said that a true sense of humor is not one's ability to laugh. A true sense of humor is one's ability to laugh at oneself.

If you were to ask, "Laura, what is the one thing about Jay that irritates you?" she would have to answer, "His ability to laugh in the middle of an argument!"

We will be fussing and fuming, arguing and yelling, and with no warning at all, this big cheesy grin comes across his face, one of those grins that you can't help but grin at yourself.

"Don't grin," responds my brain. And then he does it! He laughs, and it's all over. My brain gives in.

I laugh. My brain is on overload. I think I am mad, My face is grinning, not an angry response. My brain shuts down. I can't remember why I was mad in the first place!

Laughter in marriage can change an attitude of anger into one of joy...or forgetfulness!

Thoughts: _____
_____
_____
_____

Action Step: _____
_____

September 22

Laughter changes your perspective.

Sometimes all we need is a new perspective, a new way of seeing an issue, or a conflict, or our spouse! Laughter can perform that metamorphosis in a marriage.

Martin Luther once stated, "I judge the depth of a man's faith by his ability to laugh." How true.

Whenever we have a conflict, we ask this question--will this matter in 100 years?

In marriage, there are times when issues arise that will make a difference in 100 years. Those issues cannot be solved with laughter. The solution in these situations lies in hard work and faith in God that is more powerful than any issue.

On the other hand, how we roll the toilet paper can be a laughable argument that can change our perspective....and how we see the toilet paper unrolling!

Perspective is something we all have and at times in marriage there are two different perspectives between husband and wife!

And sometimes laughter can change one or both perspectives!

Thoughts: _____

_____

_____

Action Step: _____

_____

September 23

Laughter changes your heart!

In Proverbs 4:23 (NIV), Solomon reminds us, "Above all else, guard your heart, for it is

the wellspring of life." Laughter can help us forget about the troubles that surround us.

Laughter literally reaches deep within us and changes our heart. In Proverbs 17:22 (NIV), Solomon wrote, "A cheerful heart is good medicine, but a crushed spirit dries up the bones."

When laughter becomes an integral part of our marriage, we expose our lives to a healing power that will help us realize the potential growth God intended us to experience as a couple.

When we intentionally build times of laughter into our lives, it is like taking a daily swig of

castor oil—without the lousy taste. We begin to experience all of the benefits.

Having a date with your spouse that includes something fun to spark laughter. Sit down and watch a funny movie together will create a time of laughter. Even if you are a very serious person, laughter is something you need to do with your spouse!

Thoughts: _____

_____

_____

_____

Action Step: _____

_____

September 24

Here are some tips for adding laughter to your life and marriage:

- Spend some time recalling some humorous moments in your marriage. You may need to look at pictures or check out your Facebook posts--for some reason we post funny times there!
- Take in a funny movie or play. If you don't normally go to movies--like us--ask a friend for a recommendation.
- Create your own video comedy marathon. With Netflix this is a easy thing to do.
- Read funny books together. Or subscribe to a clean joke of the day email and share it with your spouse.
- Have a laughing party at the dinner table. Don't be afraid to allow laughter at the table. It is great for kids to see mom and dad having a good belly laugh!

Well, we hope we have encouraged you to laugh a lot in your marriage! Laughter changes your heart, your perspective, your attitude and last but not least, your chemistry!

Go ahead…laugh!

Thoughts: _____
_____
_____
_____

Action Step: _____
_____

September 25

As a married couple, play is an integral part of your relationship

"You learn more about someone through an hour of play than through an hour of conversing." -Plato

Ladies, remember when you started dating? You may have never attended a sporting event in your life, but if your boyfriend liked sports, you liked sports. Why? Because we all seek companionship in relationships.

When we marry, we feel we have found that someone. Then life happens, and it is as if when we stood at the altar and said, "I do" promise to love, honor and cherish, we say "I don't," to sports, hunting, cars. Sadly, we begin to do our own thing.

One reason women have girlfriends to have lunch or shop with, and men have golfing or hunting buddies, is that when we play, we communicate on a different level.

Seek activities that you and your spouse can do together, that you both enjoy, and "play" together. This is a great way to communicate to the body, mind, and soul of your mate.

Thoughts: _____
_____
_____
_____

Action Step: _____
_____

September 26

My man is my mission field!

We all have at one time or another served in a mission type activity whether it is a soup kitchen, volunteering to serve in our church, or a trip overseas. But do we consider how we can serve our spouse?

As our good friend Ken Davis shares, love is spelled T.I.M.E. When we give of our time, we serve our wives and children. I am convinced that, despite what Hollywood would have us believe, most ladies would rather have time with their husbands than more money. Also, I believe they would choose their husband's presence over their presents.

Americans have discovered that there are only 24 hours in a day, and with all of our modern conveniences and time-saving devices we still struggle to prioritize our time.

Plan time to be with your spouse, your kids, and your family, however big or small. It's a matter of service to them, and is an unquestionable expression of love that will lead to celebration.

Thoughts: _____
_____
_____

Action Step: _____
_____

September 27

"Behind every great man is a woman who thinks he hung the moon."

Jay is a firstborn son, firstborn grandson--basically a golden child. When we were married, I thought my primary calling was to keep this man humble. I proceeded for the next ten years to take this calling very seriously.

An incident in 1995, however, showed me that maybe that initial calling had been wrong. Over several years, Jay had struggled to achieve his life dream of being a speaker. Jay was boarding a plane to follow his dream, and, as he boarded the plane, Laura said, "Honey, I am proud of you."

That evening, when we talked on the phone, it was discovered that he had boarded the plane blubbering like an idiot!

"Laura, in the ten years we have been married, you have never told me you were proud of me." Wow! That calling was wrong!

Ladies, our job is not to keep our husband humble. That is the Lord's job. They need our admiration.

Thoughts: _____
_____
_____

Action Step: _____
_____

September 28

Love is about playing together, serving each other, speaking each other's love language and giving each other respect.

Here are a few tips for making that happen:

- Talk about the expressions of love. Do they ring true? Do you play together? Do you take time to serve each other? Are you trying to speak your spouse's love language? Do you show respect?

- Evaluate yourself and your spouse on how well you express love. Take each of those areas and give yourselves a rating. 1-10, not so good to great! Be honest in your evaluations. The hard work will pay off in the end.

- Set a realistic goal—one "expression" that needs work. What specifically can be done to improve this area of your marriage? Maybe you need to set a date to play together. Maybe time together needs to be more of a priority than it currently is.

Love is a verb! It is something we have to make a decision to do everyday--love your spouse!

Thoughts: _____
_____
_____

Action Step: _____
_____

September 29

A few summers ago, we were in Findlay, Ohio, doing a marriage seminar. Our good friend, Ken Davis, happened to join, and we thought it would be fun to go golfing together.

The first five holes went well and then the swing broke down. Laura walked off the sixth green with a ten, and she slumped into the golf cart dejected and embarrassed.

"You gotta put the bad holes behind you and play on," Jay said.

"Fine, if I am such a bad golfer you don't have to play with me anymore! I am sorry I embarrassed you in front of your friends."

What was said and what was heard were two completely different things! He had not called Laura a bad golfer. He was actually trying to be encouraging. What had been heard was entirely different.

Sound ridiculous? Yes, but don't we all do this in our marriages?

This week we focus on communication!

Thoughts: _____
_____
_____
_____

Action Step: _____
_____

September 30

"Hey Dad, what's the plan for today?"

That question was heard over and over at the Laffoon house while little ears were waiting to see when Mom or Dad were going to be available for some playtime.

For us, "the plan" is a vital link in the chain of sanity. Now, before you think there is no spontaneity in our lives, realize that "the plan" is not always set in stone. Conversation about daily life is essential. When we fail to communicate about the daily activities of the family, we open the door for little disasters that often have "Titanic" consequences.

For our family, the day-to-day planning takes place in the living room. Time management specialists state that, beginning your day at work with five solid minutes of organization will save you countless hours over the course of a year.

In marital communication as well, five minutes of planning each day will save numerous arguments and misunderstandings over the course of the day. So make your plan today!

Thoughts: _____
_____
_____

Action Step: _____
_____

October 1

We have all heard the cliche,, "The family that prays together, stays together." We have another one: "The family that plays together, stays together." We are a full-contact family. In other words, we show our affection through physical touch.

One example of our physical nature was when Torrey and Jay got down on the floor for some big-time wrestling. He always wrestled with his dad, and so it was a sort of "legacy of love on the floor" to be passed on.

What makes this time with the children so special is that it is uninterrupted. It really doesn't matter what activity you and your kids feel comfortable doing; what does matter is that they know you enjoy spending time with just them. Remember, "Love is spelled T I M E."

Thoughts: _____
_____
_____

Action Step: _____
_____

October 2

I know for most men, trivial conversation about your days events isn't on the top of your "love to-do list" especially if you work in a job with a lot of routine. It seems silly to us that our wives would care about what John and Sam ate for lunch.

However, describing the trivial details of the day's events provides your wife an avenue for understanding your world. It makes her feel a part of your life and helps her feel connected to you on a deeper level. It also becomes an effective means to practice communications skills.

Another tool to foster better communication between husband and wife involves discussing current events. Practicing communication skills while making trivial conversation will ultimately produce better skills, particularly when the communication is not so easy.

Unfortunately, most of us wait until a serious crisis arises to practice our underdeveloped techniques, which makes reciprocal communication difficult and puts added stress on the marriage, so don't be afraid to chat about the trivial.

Thoughts: _____
_____
_____

Action Step: _____
_____

October 3

"Are you two always together?"

We get that question a lot because we travel and speak together--however, early in our marriage, and even when the kids were in the house, we would serve each other by getting out of each other's hair.

There are various ways to communicate with your spouse through serving.

Laura and I give each other the freedom to enjoy different endeavors. Each of us selects one a night each week to participate in individual activities without the children and without guilt. It is important to your marriage as well as your personal growth and development to enjoy activities or hobbies that involve interaction with people who share a common interest.

Knowing that your spouse is giving you the guilt-free freedom to participate in something that stimulates you mentally, socially, spiritually, or physically is a rewarding form of service that will ultimately benefit your relationship.

Thoughts: _____
_____
_____

Action Step: _____
_____

October 4

If you could design a dream marriage, a dream lifestyle, what would it look like? Make it a B-HAG--Big Hairy Audacious Goal...why not? Are you so bogged down in the day-to-day routine that to dream anything seems too hard to imagine?

We had a dream to speak and work together helping marriages, families, and teens grow, mature, and become all God intended them to be. We also had a dream of one day writing books together. That seemed like such a long time ago but in reality the time has flown!

Dreams are important to our future, for they encourage us and give us something for which to strive. What are your dreams for today? For tomorrow? What do you want to be doing in ten years? How do you want your marriage relationship to grow over the next ten years?

Write your dreams down, put them on your fridge or on your bathroom mirror, let the written dream serve as a gentle prod to make it happen.

Thoughts: _____
_____
_____
_____

Action Step: _____
_____

October 5

5 steps to building trust in your relationship.

1) Trust Jesus. The only person you can trust without question is Jesus. You must place your trust in the Holy and Almighty God and allow Him to have control of your life.

2) Recognize that your spouse is going to let you down. The most unfair thing we can do to our spouse is to expect perfection. Setting unrealistic expectations for your spouse will only lead to heartache and frustration in your marriage.

3) Understand the forgiveness factor. Trust cannot be rebuilt until forgiveness occurs. True forgiveness is accepting your spouse's apology and moving on.

4) Speak your trust. The above three steps all happen on the inside. Now let your spouse hear that you trust him or her. Until we verbalize the things in our hearts and minds, they don't become real. Express your trust to your spouse in words.

5) Trust. Now for the action scene. Real trust initiates follow-through. Have the faith to trust.

Thoughts: _____
_____
_____
_____

Action Step: _____
_____

OCTOBER 6

Our first fight was over a sleeve of Oreo cookies! Engaged for about two months, we attended a conference with Jay's family. After a long and tiring day, we, along with Jay's sister decided to remain at the hotel for the evening. Laura wanted Oreos, but when Jay returned from the hotel lobby empty handed, the fight ensued.

"The Oreos were too expensive. I was not going to pay $3.52 for six cookies!"

What an inconsiderate slob, what a cheapskate, what a...

I can't remember who initiated the resolution, but we did resolve the conflict as we both understood the 100-year principle: "If it's not going to matter in 100 years, then it's probably not worth fighting about."

We learned a few things about each other that day--namely, he is too tight with the buck and she is spoiled!

Thoughts: _____
_____
_____

Action Step: _____
_____

October 7

A story is told of a naval captain aboard a destroyer. The morning air was filled with fog, and the crew was tense as they slipped through the icy waters. Ahead in the distance, a spotter on the bridge noticed a light that appeared to be another ship on a direct collision course with the destroyer. The captain ordered his radio operator to send word to the other ship, "We are on a collision course. Please change your heading."

A simple message returned, "You change your heading."

"This is Captain J.J. Johnson of the U.S. navy. Enough foolishness now change your heading."

"This is Ensign First Class S.D. Martin; you must change your course."

"I am the captain of a large destroyer. Now move or be struck!"

The return message was simple and clear: "Captain, I'm in a lighthouse."

All too often, our marital communication seems to be delivered in similar short unclear messages engulfed in the fog of day-to-day activity. Deliver clarity in your communication and avoid collisions!

Thoughts: _____

_____

_____

Action Step: _____

_____

October 8

Growing your marital relationship can be a challenge. Taking pro-active steps to grow your marriage will make the challenging times easier to bear. Here are some tips to grow your marriage:

First, share with your spouse your dreams…for today, for this year, for your marriage. I absolutely love when Laura starts talking about all the ways she wants to fix up our house; some are realistic and others are not, but the excitement in her voice energizes me and keeps me in love.

Second, list the different ways your spouse builds trust with you. Trust is the glue of all relationships and the more you trust your spouse the deeper you'll grow.

Finally, recall your last conflict and ask how it could have been avoided. Make sure you've given each other enough time to get over it, but learn from your mistakes. For us, this habit alone has allowed us to avoid future arguments.

Thoughts: _____
_____
_____

Action Step: _____
_____

October 9

I was conducting a teamwork seminar for a local dentist practice. The goal for the day was to discover the mission of this particular practice.

After posing the question, "June 6,1944?," a blanket of silence covered the room. People began to whisper back and forth, thinking out loud. Frank sat in the back of the room. He pioneered this practice a number of years ago, and remained physically fit for a semi-retired man in his 70s. He cleared his voice, and with a confidence found only in one who has been there, replied, "D-Day."

"What was the mission of D-Day?" Again, as Frank cleared his voice, the room sat in a silent tribute to his wisdom and knowledge. "Free Europe," was his firm response. Frank knew, as a participant in D-Day, what its mission had been--free Europe.

Have you and your spouse ever asked the question, "What is the mission of our marriage?" Over the next few days we want to help you answer that question.

Thoughts: _____
_____
_____
_____

Action Step: _____
_____

October 10

What matters to you? What matters to your spouse? Core values are simply those people, activities, beliefs, or things that matter most, ranging from concepts like love and acceptance, to something material like a home.

The first step in developing a Family Mission Statement is to list your Core Values.

Start with a manila envelope or file folder. Keep it accessible and in plain sight. Each day, write down one Core Value, and place it in the envelope. Sometimes a Core Value will become evident while you're driving to work or the store, or through a verse of song.

Don't rush the process; allow at least 30 days to collect as many values as you can. Take a Saturday morning, a Sunday evening, whenever is convenient and dump all the Core Values you have collected on a table. Categorize them by topic or any logical category that makes sense to you.

Pay particular attention to Core Values that you both wrote down. They will be a great bridge to build on in step #2.

Thoughts: _____
_____
_____

Action Step: _____
_____

OCTOBER 11

We are now moving onto step 2 in building your mission statement for your marriage, Discovering your central core value--that one thing that means the most to you both.

You have each accumulated core values. You have categorized them in a labels that make sense to you both. Now we are going to look at all those values and decide on the one thing you as a couple all want to be about.

Forever ingrained in my memory are the words."Why can't you be more like your sister?"My persistent retort echoed, "Because I am not my sister, I am me!" As a result, one of my Core Values is to be unique. Whatever I do, how I decorate my house, how I dress, how I live my life, I want to be unique. I want to be me!

After discovering that Central Core Value, you will be ready for the third step.

Thoughts: _____
_____
_____

Action Step: _____
_____

October 12

After going through the process of discovering our core values and then discussing what our central core value as a couple was, we designed Our Family Mission.

"To encourage others to become like Christ through loving relationships, healthy lifestyles, and stimulating experiences."

Let's look at our Mission Statement again. Our Central Core Value was encouraging others to become like Christ. This was the one thing we wanted to be all about. This surpassed our immediate family to include the people that we encounter every day, and through many speaking and workshop settings across the country. We accomplish this through our Core Values of loving relationships (with our family and friends), healthy lifestyles (balancing all areas of life), and stimulating experiences (a phrase which encompasses Laura's idea of uniqueness).

"To encourage others to become like Christ through loving relationships, healthy lifestyles, and stimulating experiences."

What does your mission statement look like? Start with that one thing and accomplish it through three other core values.

Thoughts: _____
_____
_____
_____

Action Step: _____
_____

October 13

We are 100 percent as disciplined as we will ever be. We're 100 percent disciplined to the good habits in our life and 100 percent disciplined to the bad habits in our life. That's depressing! The key is to develop positive personal habits to live by.

Some people call them rules, and while it may only be semantics, people don't like rules. Most of us see a list of rules, turn our back, and run because we know we can never live up to the standard of perfection we have set for ourselves.

We believe that no one is perfect and as a result, we challenge people to focus on progress, not perfection. It is amazing what this small paradigm shift can accomplish. As people focus on their progress toward positive habits, they feel a sense of accomplishment and success rather than imperfection and failure.

So take your mission statement and begin to develop positive habits that will help you accomplish the mission!

Thoughts: _____
_____
_____

Action Step: _____
_____

October 14

Are you full or empty?

Wouldn't it be great if every day we could be privy to a little gas gauge on the forehead of those around us that would let us know if they were full or empty? Life would be so much easier to handle, because then we would know why our spouse yelled at us. In many ways, however, it's fortunate that we don't have this gauge as I think far too many of us run dangerously close to empty the majority of the time.

Jesus said, "I have come that you might have life, and have it to the full" (John 10:10). Every time I read that statement, I ponder the thought of being "full" all the time.

How do you stay "full" all the time? Certainly through the Holy Spirit, but one practical step is to count your blessings. Name them out loud and thank the Lord for the many ways he has blessed you and your family and watch your tank fill up!

Thoughts: _____
_____
_____
_____

Action Step: _____
_____

OCTOBER 15

There are times when I feel my tank is empty. Most often it is the result of my own actions. I go too fast, spend too little time with the Lord, neglect family and friends, and find myself running on fumes.

How do we maintain a full life and keep our life tank from running on empty? Every married couple can find life to the full by implementing the truths found in Paul's letter to the Romans.

> *"Do not conform any longer to the pattern of this world, but be transformed by the renewing of your mind. Then you will be able to test and approve what God's will is—his good, pleasing and perfect will." (Romans 12:1-2, NIV)*

I always like to start with the end in mind, so what is the end of this verse? To test and approve what God's will is, His good, pleasing and perfect will. Now to me, if we discover God's will, then there is no way we can be anything but full.

Thoughts: _____
_____
_____

Action Step: _____
_____

October 16

So how do we transform our thinking in marriage? When he was young, our son was an expert on transformers--those little toys that look like a truck. After moving specific components, presto, you've got a robot, or an animal, or another totally different toy.

What I find interesting about transformers is that, even though the toy looks totally different from when you started, all of the parts stay the same. The same is true about transformed minds when it comes to marriage.

Christ takes us where we are and simply rearranges our perspective. He performs the transformation when we begin to realize the truth of this passage of scripture from Colossians: "Since, then, you have been raised with Christ, set your hearts on things above, where Christ is seated at the right hand of God. Set your minds on things above, not on earthly things."

The transformation that takes place is supernatural. Christ transforms the way we look at life, our spouse, and the life we have together.

Thoughts: _____

_____

_____

Action Step: _____

_____

October 17

Steven Covey states, "Character is who we are, competence is what we can do, both are necessary." In order to conform our will, we need two essential ingredients—the first being character. We must have the character to live by the decisions we have made and stand for the issues in which we believe.

The same principle is true in our marriages. We know we should date our wives, we know we shouldn't nag our husbands, we know all the "right" things that need to be done. Now the question is, will we conform our will to the pattern of this world which is constantly telling us to take the easy way out, or are we prepared to make the right choice.

The process of conforming our will involves selecting the right choices, based solely on the fact that they are the correct choices, and then act. Between thinking and acting lies the critical step of conforming our will. It takes courage. Courage is not the absence of fear, courage is fear turned inside out.

Thoughts: _____
_____
_____
_____

Action Step: _____
_____

October 18

"Offer your bodies as living sacrifices...which is your spiritual worship." There is nothing more you can do to bring about abundant life to your marriage than to offer your body. To truly serve our spouse exemplifies Christ's greatest challenge: *"Greater love has no one than this, that he lay down his life for his friends."* (John 15:13, NIV)

When was the last time you laid down your life for your spouse? When was the last time you ignored your carefully planned agenda to serve your family? You didn't seek a compromise so that you'd both get your way, but just served? For example:

"I'd take a bullet for her."

"But will you take a moment to really listen to me?"

"I'll follow him anywhere."

"Even if you disagree with my decision?"

Service is the means by which we lay down our lives for our spouse. We offer our bodies as we perform acts of service in honor of the example Christ gave us when He gave His life for us.

Thoughts: _____
_____
_____
_____

Action Step: _____
_____

October 19

Philippians 2:1: "If you have any encouragement from being united with Christ..."

Encouragement is one of the most valuable words in the English language. The word literally means "to give courage." Whether we realize it or not, when we offer encouragement, particularly to our spouse, we actually fill their tanks with the courage it may take to face a difficult task or the day at hand, or maybe just words they need to hear to brighten up their day!

Everyday we have an opportunity to encourage our spouse with words and actions. How often do we take the time to reflect on the "race" that they are running? Our encouragement may be the difference in helping them reach the summit of their particular mountain.

Every individual needs encouragement in a unique way. Ask your spouse what you do or say that gives them the encouragement they need to continue. Make a mental note to say or do those things as often as you can.

Thoughts: _____
_____
_____
_____

Action Step: _____
_____

October 20

We all stumble, we all fall--lest we forget we are human! We all have points in our lives where we cannot walk without the assistance of another human being. When we "lose" ourselves and reach out in a compassionate love, we learn the power of finishing the race together.

What is our response when we watch our spouse fall? Do we criticize? Or do we console? "But what they did hurt me!" True, it is easy for one spouse to hurt another, but I learned this lesson from my father. "Son, understand this," he said, "hurting people hurt people."

Frequently, the hurt we feel is born out of the pain experienced by the person performing the hurtful deed.

Take a moment to reflect on this passage of Scripture. "Bear with each other and forgive whatever grievances you may have against one another. Forgive as the Lord forgave you." (Colossians 3:13 NIV) What better place to practice the art of consoling (forgiveness) than with our spouse. Why do we forgive? Because the Lord has forgiven you.

Thoughts: _____
_____
_____

Action Step: _____
_____

October 21

In marriage, experiencing fellowship is critical. When we "lose" ourselves, our ambitions, our preferences, and our agendas and seek sincere fellowship, we experience a place we never want to leave. Finding this fellowship is a form of worship.

"But my spouse won't go with me to church!" is often a resounding cry. Perhaps one of the biggest of Satan's lies is that worship can take place only on Sunday morning. Worship is perpetual. We can worship God anywhere, anyplace, and anytime.

The next time you and your spouse see a beautiful sight through the window or hear an inspiring song, comment on the beauty or the depth of the words of the song, and in your spirit invite the Holy Spirit to join you. In that moment, you and your spouse will be worshiping together and your spouse may not even know it. This will be an opportunity for you to bring him or her into the presence of the Lord—the essence of all worship.

Thoughts: _____
_____
_____
_____

Action Step: _____
_____

October 22

Speaking at a mission trip in Romania, I noticed the Romanian women denote their best friend by walking in public arm in arm. If Laura and her best friend sauntered down Alma's main street locked arm in arm, they would be the talk of the town. But in Romania, it is an outward display of heartfelt affection.

Our western heritage, with all of its benefits, has really shortchanged us in the department of affection. I think we could all learn a lesson from the Romanians, and put affectionate actions back into our daily lifestyles. When we "lose" ourselves and begin to show our spouse the heartfelt love they deserve, we will win the heart of the one we love.

Ask your spouse this question: What do I do that makes you feel loved? Their answer will give you insight into the level of affection they need. (If you're real gutsy, ask them what you do that makes them feel unloved? This will shed a whole new light on your relationship.)

Thoughts: _____
_____
_____

Action Step: _____
_____

October 23

Compassion is not feeling sorry for someone. Compassion is feeling what another feels and then acting in a way that helps the person handle their particular situation. When we demonstrate compassion, we "lose" ourself in the graciousness of the act and find that, in the end, we win by creating an atmosphere where true love is shown.

Our marriages are built on mutual struggle and accomplishment, not on the back of one partner or at the expense of the other. We are united in Christ as a team to accomplish something for his kingdom, therefore:

- Encourage each other in Christ. Be your spouse's biggest fan
- Console each other in love. Be a great forgiver when the other falls
- Fellowship with each other in the Spirit. Create those moments of reflecting on God's beauty
- Demonstrate affection and compassion. Show your spouse daily affection and compassion
- Become selfless in your marriage and experience the joy of winning that "losing" brings.

Thoughts: _____
_____
_____

Action Step: _____
_____

October 24

In every marriage, the list of private issues is lengthy including job difficulties, family issues, financial concerns, church problems, social events, or surprise family activities. Whatever the case, there are times when privacy in marriage is a must.

Don't get us wrong, we are firm believers in being honest and open about the reality of life's challenges with our children; however, there are proper times and places for such explanations.

Finding a place to have those challenging conversations took some thought. For us it was the bathroom. Our children were taught that when mom and dad's bedroom or bathroom door was closed they had to knock and wait for permission to enter. Ironically the master bath became our sanctuary for tough marital discussions that didn't involve the kids.

Mom and Dad need opportunity to process their response to this issue privately. The bathroom may not be your choice for conversations with your spouse, but do find a place where you can converse freely without the intrusion of little ears.

Thoughts: _____
_____
_____
_____

Action Step: _____
_____

October 25

Communication about the future of your marriage is much like a long trip in a car. The first step is planning a destination (big picture) the second is mapping a way to get there (details). And the third and most important step is making sure the kids use the bathroom when we stop for gas or meals!

In most marriages, one person most often sees the big picture while the other focuses on the details. Jay is the personification of the big picture viewpoint, i.e. the dreamer, the visionary. He envisions fantastic dreams that seem surreal. I, on the other hand, take the big picture concept he's verbalized and draw a map taking into account the necessary steps to achieve the desired goal. If this is what we want to do honey, then this is how we need to get there. I have learned over the years that we can take any big picture vision the Lord gives Jay and turn it into a reality in our lives.

Thoughts: _____
_____
_____

Action Step: _____
_____

October 26

When traveling in life together, we offer these two simple rules: 1) Know your destination, e.g. where do you want to be financially or spiritually a year from now? and, 2) Define your roles so that each participant has a sense of self-worth and significance and contribution to the outcome.

Don't become discouraged when traffic or minor setbacks impede efficient progress toward your goal. Through patience and determination the chosen destination will soon be in view. The Lord has already seen your future and has a wonderful plan

We often find ourselves talking about the future when traveling in the car. It could be partially due to daydreaming brought on by the monotony of the white lines or merely habit.

In conversing about your family's future, you will find yourself dreaming, planning, and growing toward all that God would have you become. Take time to seek a destination towards which God is nudging you. Then carefully map out the path required to reach your goal.

Thoughts: _____
_____
_____

Action Step: _____
_____

October 27

Matthew shares, "Therefore everyone who hears these words of mine and puts them into practice is like a wise man who built his house on the rock. The rain came down, the streams rose, and the winds blew and beat against that house; yet it did not fall, because it had its foundation on the rock."

The most important type of communication a person can have is not with their spouse, it's with Jesus. Laying a foundation for communication daily with Christ will enhance and improve communication in every other area of our lives. The best thing you can do for your marriage is being in tune and on track with the Lord.

Communication manifests itself on many levels in a marriage relationship. Sometimes relating to one another is easy and other times it is extremely difficult to understand a conflicting point of view. All forms of communication can be rewarding, however. Communication is the key to celebrating your marriage throughout your lifetime together.

Thoughts: _____
_____
_____

Action Step: _____
_____

October 28

Laura and I speak for a living, write books for a living--basically, we communicate for a living and yet at times we have the hardest time communicating with each other.

All couples struggle with communication from time to time, so now might be a great time for you and your spouse to step back and make an honest evaluation of your marital communication. Here are two easy steps.

First, pick the top way you and your spouse communicate (finances, spiritual life, kids), and ask yourself why that area seems to be easier than others.

Second, take an area that really needs help and ask each other what actions need to be taken to start improvement.

Periodic evaluation of your communication as a couple will keep you growing in your marriage.

Thoughts: _____
_____
_____

Action Step: _____
_____

October 29

Do you find yourself feeling like you are on a never ending treadmill and you don't know when it will stop and throw you off? Or maybe you feel like that rodent in a cage on the running wheel that never stops!

In the first two years of our marriage, I had gained over 25 pounds as McDonalds and Taco Bell meals on the run were standard fare. Laura was either working or sleeping all the time. We were totally out of balance. Finally, upon reviewing our lifestyle, it became clear that the "rat race" had to end.

As we work with couples across the country, we see the devastating lifestyles that our demanding culture has created. If you desire to leave a legacy to your children and grandchildren, then you may realize it's time to get O.U.T.!

O - observe
U - understand
T - throw

Three actions that will help you get O.U.T. will be discussed in the next few days.

Thoughts: _____
_____
_____

Action Step: _____
_____

October 30

Observe

I call him "Pocket-change Jesus." He's the religious figure most Americans pull out of their pocket whenever they need a little help. He's like a "lucky coin," there only for our convenience.

While many of us really don't think we treat Jesus this way, the truth is we have no idea of the majesty of our Lord. He is truly "Big Jesus" and we should stand in awe, wonder, and fear.

The first step in getting out of the rat race and really enjoying marriage is to observe the greatness of our God. We must understand that Jesus is the great Creator God Almighty. He spoke and the universe spun into place. "Let there be" and there was—the universe and everything in it as a testimony to the Creator.

Stop for a moment and observe the greatness of our God. He is mighty, magnificent, and majestic. Observing His greatness will strike a holy fear which the psalmist says is the "beginning of wisdom." (111:10 NIV)

Thoughts: _____
_____
_____
_____

Action Step: _____
_____

October 31

Understand

Most of us spend our time either running from a past we cannot change or running toward a future that is uncertain, instead of running with God, the giver of life. We must admit we are totally powerless over sin so we can truly begin to allow God's Spirit to work in us and demonstrate the meaning of a full life.

The second step in getting out of the rat race is to understand our sin. Sin is just our nature. We must recognize the need to battle sin every day, particularly in our marriage.

Virtually every day our sin nature will cause us to act selfishly or in a hurtful manner. Understanding our sin allows us to admit that we are powerless over it and as we daily surrender that weakness, we allow the grace of God to flow through us, making us more like Christ.

Marriage is the perfect proving ground for living a life of undenied weakness and reliance on the Lord as the source of our strength.

Thoughts: _____
_____
_____

Action Step: _____
_____

November 1

Throw

Laura and I have survived two major household moves. Each time we moved, I was overwhelmed by the junk that we had accumulated. We would find ourselves holding up a something or other and ask, "What in the world is this?" My textbook retort, "Throw it out!"

Wouldn't it be nice if it were that easy to throw out the junk, the garbage, and the unnecessary baggage in our marriages?

Why not sit down with your spouse and make a list of those things that have crept into your marriage. Take a "junk inventory" and see what can be thrown out. The "junk" could include habits or actions that you have fallen into as a couple that have been detrimental to your relationship.

Some couples have a routine of going to bed at different times. For some, that may not be a bad thing; however, for us that would create havoc. If I went to bed every night at eight o'clock and read until I feel asleep, we would never spend any time alone!

Throw it out!

Thoughts: _____
_____
_____
_____

Action Step: _____
_____

November 2

Linger longer

The word "linger" brings to mind the picture of a wide front porch with huge rocking chairs, a warm breeze, and two people enjoying each other's company. That is what God designed us to do in our marriages. Take time to linger with your spouse. Take time to enjoy each other. Get out and sit on the front porch. Feel the breeze blow in your face and linger together!

Why not...

- Take some time away in nature and reconnect with the Creator. Observe the Creator God who brought you together.
- Tell your spouse you are sorry for any hurt you have caused today. Understand you are going to sin and say hurtful things but acknowledging and asking forgiveness goes a long way.
- Make a list of the "junk" in your marriage that you are responsible for and then throw it out.

Lingering together allows us to enjoy each and other and our marriage as God created it to be enjoyed! So linger a bit longer...

Thoughts: _____
_____
_____

Action Step: _____
_____

November 3

Lead, follow or get out of the way!

That was a phrase my father used often as I was growing up. He said he learned it in the army while in boot camp. The drill sergeant was tasked with developing leaders and that was the phrase he used if he thought one of the soldiers was slacking off.

One of the best definitions of leadership I've ever heard is, "leadership equals influence." Your ability to lead your spouse depends on your ability to influence those around you.

One of the best illustrations of this came from the movie My Big Fat Greek Wedding. The daughter getting married was distraught because her father had "put his foot down" on some wedding details so she was crying and being comforted by her mom.

Her mom said, "The man is the head of the house but the woman is the neck and can turn that head in any direction she chooses." Leadership equals influence!

Thoughts: _____
_____
_____

Action Step: _____
_____

November 4

Your marriage will journey through four stages. The first stage is the honeymoon stage--we are in love; neither person can do anything wrong and forgiveness comes easy. Your heart skips a beat every time your loved one enters the room.

As the relationship grows, the second stage, chaos, develops. The children have arrived. Your marriage is maturing, becoming settled. Routines begin to solidify. Your heart may not always skip a beat when your love walks into the room.

The third stage, "to be emptied." We have to come to a point in our lives when we say "it isn't all about me." We have to put aside our individual agendas, desires, and needs to focus on our partner.

Then, and only then, will we achieve unity, the fourth stage. In this stage, we must strive to work together rather than against each other.

Leadership in marriage is about both partners leading and both following. Leadership is not about who is strongest or smartest or loudest; it's about who is willing to be led.

Thoughts: _____
_____
_____

Action Step: _____
_____

November 5

Leadership is found in humility.

I was never more humbled than at a leadership training retreat. We were playing a game called "Out of the Pits." On the sound of, "go," one student laid down on his back. As quickly as the group could, they lifted that student to head height, and then lowered him gently to the floor. In the middle of playing this game I was feeling cocky and arrogant as we bent down to lift a particularly large man off the floor. Rip! It wasn't a gentle tearing of the garment. It was a stem-to-stern rip of my shorts.

Terror struck my heart in anticipation of the coming dilemma. You see, I was in a classroom full of youth leaders and everyone of them knew exactly what just happened. My shorts were torn and I stood in front of this class of leaders baring it all.

Life will humble us all so we might as well choose, as Christ did, to humble ourselves. In the long run it's a lot less embarrassing. And you can't lead others until you have been humbled!

Thoughts: _____
_____
_____
_____

Action Step: _____
_____

November 6

A young woman was preparing to be a missionary to West Africa. As she prepared to go she visited garage sales to stock up on items she could take with her. At one sale, she distinctly heard the voice of God tell her to buy some soccer balls.

When she arrived at the school, she entered a prayer meeting. As the missionary woman listened, she heard one boy shout out "soccer balls!" Another boy stood up praying for soccer balls, pleading their need for soccer balls for recess.

She rose from her seat and went back to her room and retrieved the soccer balls that she had brought. As she entered the room where the boys were praying she tripped and the soccer balls fell out of her arms and down the center aisle. The boys were astonished! "How did God do that?!"

In marriage God will ask us to do some things that seem odd at the time, but in his timing our obedience will bear fruit!

Thoughts: _____
_____
_____

Action Step: _____
_____

November 7

My Mom had slipped on the ice, and a fraction of a second later, her foot hit a clean patch of pavement. The force and torque of her movements were so violent, that she broke her leg in ten places between her knee and her ankle. Daily, Dad had the arduous task of cleaning the 14 pin sites that stuck out of her leg.

Morning and evening, in his pursuit of serving his wife, Dad would sit on his knees with Mom's leg in front of him and two bright lights shining over his shoulders. Cleaning the pin sites was a 30-minute process as three separate cleaning solutions were used on each site.

Finally, nine months after the accident, the pins were removed.

What we saw in my dad was a true heart of a servant. My mom couldn't put any weight on her leg so my dad literally did everything around the house while holding down his job and nursing his wife back to health.

Serving is leading...and loving your spouse!

Thoughts: _____
_____
_____
_____

Action Step: _____
_____

November 8

Marriage involves leading, but being led as well. Sometimes that is a lot easier said than done!

I am the third of four children, two girls and two boys. There is some truth to the birth order theories! Sandy is definitely a firstborn. She is the boss. She is the meticulous one. She is the example the rest of us were supposed to follow. Greg is quiet, usually did his own thing, and really never bothered anybody. Tom is the typical baby of the family. He has had lots of practice batting those big blue eyes and getting whatever he wants. I am the third born child, lost in the crowd.

My sister and I are very different people. Growing up, I realized then that in order to survive, blazing my own trail was unavoidable and I became very independent. Blazing your own trail is all well and good, until you want your trail to merge with another's.

Marriage is about merging those two trails together and leading and being led at different times.

Thoughts: _____
_____
_____
_____

Action Step: _____
_____

November 9

Merging two trails together means submitting.

The Apostle Paul writes "Honor Christ by submitting to each other's leadership. You wives must submit to your husband's leadership in the same way you submit to the Lord."

That verse starts out sounding good…we submit to each other… then Paul singles us out! "You wives…." I think that he knew this was going to be hard for us.

But this doesn't mean you live trampled underfoot like a doormat. Notice the first part of the verse says that we honor Christ by submitting to each other's leadership. There will be times your wife will know the best course of action. In our house, I am the barometer. I seem to know best when we need family time, or when Jay and I need some time alone. Jay listens to me and respects my leadership in these areas. We need to honor each other by recognizing those gifts and allowing each other to lead with their unique gifts.

Thoughts: _____
_____
_____
_____

Action Step: _____
_____

November 10

Ephesians 5:23: "For a husband is in charge of his wife in the same way Christ is in charge of his body the church." I can hear you...no one is in charge of me but me! Not true. If you call yourself a Christian, you gave those controls over to Jesus.

If you were to look up "charge" in the dictionary you would see the words "responsible," "safekeeping," "care," and "trust" are all a part of the definition. Now that doesn't sound so bad! Why do we always have to read this passage and think negative thoughts?

The rest of the passage reads, "Husbands, love your wives, just as Christ loved the church and gave himself up for her." (Ephesians 5:25 NIV)

We must develop the ability to appreciate life from the half-full point of view instead of half-empty. Rejoice in the command the Lord has given us for our marriages. We are being taken care of out of love.

Thoughts: _____
_____
_____

Action Step: _____
_____

November 11

"For a husband is in charge of his wife in the same way Christ is in charge of his body the church." I can hear you…no one is in charge of me but me!

Bear with me please…If you were to look up the word "charge" in the dictionary you would see the words "responsible," "safekeeping," "care," and "trust" are all a part of the definition. Jesus is telling me that I am responsible for Laura, I am to keep her safe, and to care for her.

Jay frequently likes to joke with that I'm a "kept woman." When I was growing up, my image of a "kept woman" was someone who sat around and ate bon-bons, went to the club for lunch, spent the rest of the day shopping, and went home at night to lounge in a bubble bath! Now, before you think that is what I do, let me set you straight. I don't like bon-bons! Seriously, allow your husband to be responsible for you and be "kept" too!

Thoughts: _____
_____
_____

Action Step: _____
_____

November 12

Leading.
Being Led.
Following.
Being humbled, emptied.
Submitting.

Trying to implement all these concepts into our marriage can be confusing and difficult.

Sp why not read Ephesians, chapter 5 together and pray, asking the Lord to give you His insight. Discover for yourself what you think the Lord is saying to you about leadership in your marriage. Discuss the roles that have emerged in your marriage. Are you leading and following?

What ones are good? What ones need improving? Does one of you lead better than the other? Do either of you follow the other when necessary?

Discuss how your marriage aligns with the Ephesians chapter. Are you serving each other? Are you being responsible for each other and the state of your marriage, or are you coasting along each doing your own thing?

Why not take some time to evaluate your marriage according to Ephesians 5.

Thoughts: _____
_____
_____
_____

Action Step: _____
_____

November 13

The phone rang at 3 p.m. and my mom sounded concerned; "Jay, the doctor called and he wants to see me in his office. Jay, it can't be good news if he wants to see me in his office!"

When the telephone it rang again at 5:30 p.m, Mom said, "Six weeks...the doctor said I have only six weeks to live..." What they found was a metastasized malignant melanoma, the deadliest form of cancer.

In God's providential way, six weeks to the day after getting her prognosis, the doctors declared my mother cancer free! That was 20 years ago, and she's still cancer free.

My mom said, "You know, in six weeks, I could be dead…gone… pushing up daisies. But if that is the case, then I just have one thing to say to each and every one of you…I'll be with Jesus, and in a whole lot better condition than any of you."

Her legacy was simple: Follow Jesus.

What legacy is your life, your marriage leaving?

Thoughts: _____
_____
_____

Action Step: _____
_____

November 14

I am the son of a minister who was in the military. Therefore I do nothing in this world without guilt or fear! Growing up my father always said: "Jay, if you're five minutes early, you're on time. If you're on time, you're late, and if you're late, you're rude!"

I asked my dad why he always made that statement. He told me: "Son, you will be late from time to time, But, if you live your life always running late and always making others wait for you, you are telling the rest of the world that your time is more valuable than theirs, and son, that is just plain rude."

If you want to leave a legacy that points people to Christ, start with treating all the people in your world with respect. One way to show that respect is to consider others' time as valuable as your own. Make your marriage a union that honors each other by helping each other be punctual. If you tend to perpetually run late, then ask your spouse to help you manage your time better.

Thoughts: _____
_____
_____

Action Step: _____
_____

November 15

I wish I could say that I've used the words "please" and "thank you" every day.

I was flying through Chicago O'Hare and, on a layover, entered one of those concession stands where you can get a hot dog and a Coke for $18.00 (small exaggeration!). Standing in line behind a flight attendant, we both filled our Coke cups. She reached for a lid, and two stuck together. Instinctively, she separated them and handed one to me. I looked her in the eye and simply said, "Thank you." She whipped around and gave me a surprised look.

Stunned, I said "Hey, I'm sorry, I didn't mean anything." "No, I'm sorry." She said, "I just got off a plane with 182 passengers, not one of them said thank you!"

We live in an incredibly rude society. One of the best ways we can leave a legacy, pointing people to Christ, is to stand out as unique and different by challenging each other to practice simple politeness.

Thoughts: _____
_____
_____

Action Step: _____
_____

November 16

I enjoy watching the shows on HGTV where the host can make a magnificent holiday centerpiece out of two pinecones and some twine. Amazingly, nothing is wasted. It drives me crazy because I'm a waster.

Every trash day I lament how much our family throws out. I promise to do better and will do well for a while, and then boom! I open the refrigerator to find 18 colorful Tupperware bowls filled with moss green food in various stages of decomposition. My stomach turns and I don't know if it's from the smell or from the realization that our fridge is just a small reflection of a larger, more disturbing, issue—stewardship.

Jesus spoke more about money than almost any other issue. "For where your treasure is, there your heart will be also." (Matthew 6:21 NIV) His words cut to the quick when we realize how much we've been given, compared to how we often misuse it.

Stand out, be different, be practical as a good steward, and leave a legacy that will point others to Christ.

Thoughts: _____
_____
_____
_____

Action Step: _____
_____

November 17

Little eyes and ears watch and hear everything you say. If you want to leave a legacy, be purposeful and do what you say!

I learned to snow ski at an early age. I told Laura we were going to be a skiing family. At three, our son Torrey hit the the slopes. For the next few years we had no snow; however, the year Torrey was nine, the snow was abundant and we returned to our favorite winter activity.

As we rode up the chair lift Torrey said, "Dad, I'm glad you finally kept your word." "What do you mean, kept my word?" "Well Dad, I remember you saying that we would always be a skiing family, and for the last three years we haven't skied. Now we are, I'm glad you kept your word." For all those years he'd remembered. All too often we do not realize the impact of what we say.

As a result, we must be purposeful in all that we say and do. If we are to leave a legacy that points other people to Jesus, we must live a purposeful life.

Thoughts: _____
_____
_____

Action Step: _____
_____

November 18

Think back to what it was that first attracted you to your spouse. You may have met participating in a sport, hobby, or class. You may have met on a blind date. Whatever the scenario, marriage resulted because you enjoyed being with each other. You liked each other and you became and remain friends.

In order to celebrate your marriage, you've got to like each other. Now I know that some of you hearing this right now are saying, "Like? Friends? You gotta be kidding. We hardly even cross paths anymore, what with our jobs, our children, our hobbies; our committee involvements. How are we supposed to be friends?"

This week, we're going to share four important habits that will keep your friendship alive and well while living out this thing called marriage. These habits are:

Find commonalities

Carve out time

Never quit growing

Become a sequoia tree

Building these habits into your marriage will grow your friendship and strengthen your bond creating a best friend for life!

Thoughts: _____
_____
_____
_____

Action Step: _____
_____

NOVEMBER 19

Finding activities in common can be difficult at times in marriage but pursuing commonalities will keep the friendship alive.

I love golf! Love to watch golf and love to play golf. Laura never had much time for golf. "Stupid game!" she would remark as I watched the Masters Tournament being televised at beautiful Augusta National on Sunday afternoon.

Laura would find the time to play a round with me under the guise of a fun summertime "date." The occasional good hole or excellent shot proved to be just the "come backer" she needed to stay with the game.

It all came together when Laura's friend Beth asked if she wanted to attend golf school. So off went my little weekend hacker. Back came my dream girl! The love of my life now shares my most passionate hobby.

It is a tribute to her flexibility and willingness to learn that has given us golf as a common interest. Now she says all I have to do is learn to love to shop!

Thoughts: _____
_____
_____

Action Step: _____
_____

November 20

We recommend you make finding uninterrupted time together a priority. Find creative ways to date.

If child care is a concern, it is money well spent to hire a babysitter and invest time in your relationship. There are two reasons for this: 1) Children need to observe healthy male/female relationships. If Mom and Dad don't go out on dates, what motivation will they have to develop a healthy dating relationship of their own? If all the kids see are Mom and Dad flopped on the couch each night or, just as bad, working till all hours, where will they gain an appreciation for healthy interaction with other human beings? 2) All too soon our children will be graduating from high school or college and move out of the house to begin their own lives. Maintaining a close friendship with our spouse during the child-rearing years will build a strong relationship and prepare us for the "empty nest" years ahead.

So put a date on your calendar today!

Thoughts: _____
_____
_____
_____

Action Step: _____
_____

November 21

There is something new to learn every day. If we stop learning, we stop growing. Jay is learning something new about me every day!

Learn a new hobby. I am learning to grow flowers in our yard. After purchasing a promising yellow rosebush, I soon found myself exploring the Internet to learn the latest technique to promote successful growth. Though I followed the instructions to the letter, it collapsed before my eyes! I discovered that starting with a rosebush to learn to grow flowers was not the best idea!

Installing a bird feeder in our backyard has provided an opportunity for our family to learn about the birds that migrate in our locale. Everyday we look forward to watching the various species munch on the seeds we've provided. We have discovered that if we put different bird seed in the feeder, different types of birds are attracted to dine at our table.

There is so much uncharted territory in our world, our lives, and our spouse's lives that await discovery! Life is an adventure…we can never stop growing!

Thoughts: _____
_____
_____
_____

Action Step: _____
_____

November 22

The magnificent white pine grows to heights of nearly 150 feet and has a tap root that grows as deep into the Michigan sand as the tree stands high. Many of us see ourselves as having deep roots that allow us to firmly "stand alone" against all odds. In truth, we are very different. In fact, we were not meant to stand alone.

The amazing giant sequoia tree reaches a height of over 300 feet... for its massive size the sequoia has an incredibly shallow root system as the roots reach a depth of only five or six feet. How then does this tree stand secure against the fierce Pacific storms and winds? Simple. You will never see a sequoia stand alone. Their roots become intertwined with other sequoias and gain tremendous strength. What a perfect picture of how we should grow together as a couple.

Marriage is the perfect place to practice that reliance—by growing together as a couple.

Thoughts: _____
_____
_____

Action Step: _____
_____

November 23

Remember how the emotions and feelings you had when you first fell in love? You'd get that ooey gooey liver quiver, couldn't wait to be with each other. The touch of your spouse's hand sent shivers down your spine and when you kissed...oh my, we were in "love."

Science is now revealing that "love" is actually a product of our biology. Certainly "love" hormones like oxytocin and dopamine are released when we are falling in love. Seriously, dopamine? Could there be a better word for a love hormone?

The problem is that, with time, these hormones don't get released as often or in as large of quantity. And in time, dopamine is replace by the hormone did I marry a dope?

Love is understanding that over time we must make a conscious choice about doing those things that we were once driven to do by infatuation and the hormones it produces. So fondly remember the love you shared early on and make the conscious choice to feel that way today.

Thoughts: _____

_____

_____

Action Step: _____

_____

November 24

Laura and I met on a blind date. July 4th, 1984, Atlanta Braves baseball game, accompanied by fireworks. I must've made quite an impression, because Laura told her mom the next day that she was going to marry me! She definitely made an impression on me, because 10 days later on July 14th, 1984, I asked her to be my wife!

It was a whirlwind romance and we were on the ride of our life! I didn't have a ring but made plans to give her one exactly one month later on top of Soldiers Mountain in Woodland Park, Colorado. When I presented the ring standing at 12,000 feet above sea level I hadn't factored for the altitude, and as a result instead of Laura saying yes, she regurgitated her lunch all over me!

We tell our story to remind couples that marriage has it's mountaintop and messy moments! So remember when the messes come that the mountaintop is just around the corner!

Thoughts: _____
_____
_____
_____

Action Step: _____
_____

November 25

Intimacy is something we all long for because it is powerful and life changing. It is also elusive. We don't know when it will show up or how long it will last. In fact, no one understands intimacy when they fall in love. We sure didn't. Intimacy is the spark. The spark starts small and grows with time into a burning flame of love. Over the years, how that fire is stoked will determine the depth, and joy experienced in a relationship.

To keep the fires of love alive, careful attention must be paid to all facets of intimacy. We believe that there are five facets of intimacy: social, mental, emotional, physical, and spiritual intimacy. Each of these facets is key to igniting the passion, romance, and mystery in your marriage.

Intimacy is often misunderstood. We want to help you understand it by looking at these five facets--but first, we have to lay some ground work that involves looking at the priority your marriage plays in your life as well as defining some common terms.

Thoughts: _____

_____

_____

Action Step: _____

_____

November 26

My friend, Joe, mentioned something in passing that hit me like a slap on the face. Joe said, "Here are my priorities: 1. God, 2. My wife, 3. My children." In that moment I realized we have our priorities screwed up!

Ask a typical Christian to share their priorities and they will say, "1. God, 2. Family." Do you see the slight but essential difference in what Joe said and what most of us would say?

Here is where we make our mistake: not realizing that our relationship with our spouse is completely distinct from our relationship with our children and the rest of our family. our first and primary relationship after God is with our spouse. Our wrongly configured priorities materialize in many dysfunctional ways:

- Parents who dive into work instead of diving into each other.
- Parents who spend all their time chauffeuring or coaching or watching children play insane amounts of sports or other activities.

The single best thing you can do for your child outside of having an authentic walk with Christ is to make your marriage a priority.

Thoughts: _____
_____
_____
_____

Action Step: _____
_____

November 27

We believe the key to unlocking celebration in your marriage begins with something we all desire—intimacy. It is the building and developing of intimacy that will help you celebrate your marriage.

We can all look at our spouses and see what we wish we could change. Marriage is accepting those idiosyncrasies and not spending too much energy on changing that which we cannot.

When you are young and you watch a romantic movie, you really think that is what life will be like! You watch a TV husband and wife sleeping all cozy next to each other, appearing to be the perfect couple, When the TV couple awakens, they open their eyes looking at each other while adoringly smiling and kissing good morning. What a crock of hooey! What about morning breath, bed-head hair, and those lovely morning volcanic eruptions from that perfect man or woman next to you!

Being married is accepting the things we would rather change!

Thoughts: _____
_____
_____

Action Step: _____
_____

November 28

We love to ask couples, "What is the purpose of marriage?" Some of you may already be answering that question in your head. You may be coming up with all different kinds of answers: procreation, companionship, fun, to find a "sugar-daddy" or a "mommy-dearest," or if you're really spiritual, you might be saying that the purpose of marriage is to become like Christ.

We believe Jesus tells us the purpose of marriage in Mark 10:6-8. "But at the beginning of creation, God made them male and female. For this reason, a man will leave his father and mother and be united to his wife and the two will become one flesh."

Up to this point, Jesus is quoting the Old Testament. But then Jesus closed His quote on the Old Testament and gave the purpose of marriage: "So, they are no longer two, but one." The purpose of marriage, then, according to Jesus Christ Himself, is to be one.

This week we unpack what it means to be one.

Thoughts: _____
_____
_____
_____

Action Step: _____
_____

November 29

Oneness is the perception which comes from sharing daily duties together. Being one is a state of the heart, soul, and mind.

A great way to discern the difference between "oneness" and "being one" is to understand the difference between "the institutional aspects of marriage" and "the mysterious aspects of marriage."

As we look at couples practicing the "institution" we find people who live in the same house, pay the same bills, raise the same kids, maybe even "go out" to the same movie together. While practicing these institutional aspects of marriage may bring a feeling of oneness, it does not answer some of the deeper questions.

While the "institution" of marriage is mostly practical, figuring out who will pay the bills, do the grocery shopping, mow the lawn, clean the house, the "mystery" of marriage is more of an art. The art is revealed as we discover the heart, soul and mind of our spouse and, at the same time reveal ours in order to probe the depths of emotion, character and love; which is truly being one.

Thoughts: _____

_____

_____

Action Step: _____

_____

November 30

The NCAA Division I football championship, 1986, was going to be decided between two very different teams. the number one ranked Hurricanes from Miami of Florida were a flashy, superstar ridden, offensive juggernaut putting up an average of 38 points a game. Number two ranked Nittany Lions of Penn State were the boring uniformed midwestern version of a blue collar plodder.

Miami came out with the names of the players embroidered on the backs of their uniforms. This made it easy to identify which superstar was making what amazing play. Penn State came out in their drab white and black and it struck me that there were no names on the back of their jerseys. I turned to Laura and said. "Penn State is going to win this one because they are a team."

The Nittany Lions prevailed 14-10.

So what does this have to do with being one? Plenty. You see, when you put on the "uniform" in marriage you put on a uniform that has no names on the back, no superstar husbands or Heisman trophy wives. You are one.

Thoughts: _____
_____
_____
_____

Action Step: _____
_____

December 1

Ever try to explain marriage to a single person? It's tough…it's like the married people are in a giant swimming pool trying to get the single people to jump in…come on it's great…well it looks wavy, oh it's wavy…it looks deep…oh it's deep…it looks cold…you get used to it!

John Piper writes: "marriage is a mystery — it contains and conceals a meaning far greater than what we see on the outside. God created man male and female and ordained marriage so that the eternal covenant relationship between Christ and his church would be imaged forth in the marriage union."

So, the bad news is that if God created marriage as a mystery, then no one will ever figure it out…yikes! The good news is that, as we grow together and walk this journey together, God reveals new portions of the mystery to us.

As God does this he shows us more of ourselves, more of our spouse, and most importantly more of Him!

Thoughts: _____
_____
_____

Action Step: _____
_____

December 2

How do we achieve being one?

Dance.

The only way you can dance is if you are living in the moment. You don't dance in the past; you don't dance in the future; you dance right now. A couple dancing can dance as two separate individuals stepping on toes, not sure who is leading, looking uncomfortable and awkward. Or, a couple can dance as two individuals who have come together intentionally, moving together as one, each doing their part of the dance seamlessly, meshed together, music in motion.

Fire dances too! We have all sat around a campfire, entranced by the dancing flames. Separate those flames by breaking up the logs, and the flame soon dies. The same is true with the spark of intimacy.

The five facets of intimacy are like the logs of a fire. As we intertwine, our lives the flame grows and the fire burns brighter. Time to set your marriage ablaze!

Thoughts: _____
_____
_____

Action Step: _____
_____

December 3

I suspect many of us have never thought about being socially intimate with our spouses. In fact, we frequently received this answer: "I'm not sure what you mean by social intimacy."

We begin dating and we enjoy this person's companionship. We have common interests. We are friends. Then somewhere along the line we fall in love. For some it happens quickly, for others over time, we discover that we've become more than friends. We become husband and wife.

For some reason when this happens, very often, we cease being friends. Here are some reasons: "Time mostly--not making our date time a priority." "Making the time. We have it, just don't make it." "I usually spend my time alone, usually associated with work."

As the marriage begins. Life settles in, careers, a mortgage and obligations. Children are born, more obligations. Careers take off, and responsibilities rise. Suddenly we discover that our friendship as well as the time to nurture it no longer exists.

We must remember to create time to nurture our friendship with our spouse.

Thoughts: _____

_____

_____

Action Step: _____

_____

December 4

I grew up in a home with a diabetic dad and, as a result, ate meat and potatoes growing up. Food, for me, was simple and plain.

Jay, on the other hand, grew up in a home where food was an event. It was to be taken seriously and always an opportunity to try something new. It didn't matter where it came from, just how it tasted!

We figured out quickly food was going to be a struggle.

One day we are driving in the middle of nowhere and were starving. We stumble across a mom and pop Mexican restaurant.

I agreed to go in. The chips and salsa were homemade and the cuisine some of the finest to be found. I exclaimed, "So this is Mexican?" You see, it wasn't that I didn't like ethnic food. It was that I had never even tried it!

Social intimacy begins by blending many of the interests of your two lives into one. One area we had to blend was Jay's "international palette" with Laura's "cautious palette".

Thoughts: _____
_____
_____
_____

Action Step: _____
_____

December 5

One of my favorite characters the comedian, Johnny Carson, used to perform was "Carnac the Magnificent." He could magically answer the question in the "sealed" envelope by simply holding the envelope up to his forehead. The secret to Carnac's success was to always be "one ahead." Johnny would pre-arrange the answer to the first envelope before the show. After successfully answering the question before it was asked he would rip open the envelope and reveal the question.

Staying one ahead is a great way to keep your dating life alive. We see this principle fleshed out each year at our marriage conferences as we will have roughly 1/3 of the couples attending sign up for next year's conference before they leave the current one. They are "planning" social time into their marriage.

Staying one ahead is a great way to keep your marriage "tuned-up." So as you finish one weekend or night or even afternoon away, begin planning your next so you too can stay "one ahead."

Thoughts: _____
_____
_____

Action Step: _____
_____

December 6

Harry and Donna attended every sporting event of their children. They were so consumed with their children's sports schedules that they never had time left for just themselves as a couple.

Barbara works full time outside the home. Daily chores are done after work and she spends her weekends catching up on the larger household tasks. Barbara feels as if she never has time to go out with her husband.

Detractors hinder growth: finances, housework, family needs, work load, money, energy, kids' sports schedules.

Attractors enable growth: "date nights," shared activities, developing mutual hobbies, doing even menial errands together, vacations, getaways, meals out.

Ralph and Julie have been married for 41 years and are still best friends. If you asked if it has always been this way, they would tell you no. It has taken hard work and effort.

As time has gone by and they have grown as individuals and as a couple they have realized the importance of doing things together.

Thoughts: _____
_____
_____
_____

Action Step: _____
_____

December 7

We all can identify with the fact that we think differently than our spouse! For example, when Jay says "let's go into the city", he means, "Let's go test drive cars". I (Laura) think he means, "Let's go shopping at the mall"! When I say, "let's take a nap", I mean, "let's sleep". Jay thinks I am saying...well we won't go there...

Others who have recognized their differences put it this way:

I am much more intellectually driven. I enjoy learning. He considers himself to be inferior to me in that area.

I have more "book smarts," he has more "street smarts."

As we grow closer, we understand each other so much more

Becoming mentally intimate means living by this quote: "It's not how smart you are, it's how you are smart." That bears repeating... it's not how smart you are, it's how you are smart!

Everyone has intelligence, smart couples learn to love and lean on each others intelligence, realizing that two heads are better than one!

Thoughts: _____
_____
_____
_____

Action Step: _____
_____

December 8

It really didn't take me long to figure out that Laura's brain operated very differently from mine. I remember moving into our first apartment and watching in amazement as she took her socks from a moving box and put them into her sock drawer... she simply opened the box and threw them into the drawer. I was appalled--you see, God has a plan for socks. We serve a God of order. Even Noah collected animals two by two: a simple lesson for the sock drawer!

Over the years I tried in a variety of ways to show her how a sock drawer should look, but to no avail. Finally I realized that the way Laura kept her sock drawer was simply a function of the way her mind works. My mind is linear: step one, step two, step three. Laura's is random: steps, what steps?

Neither way is right or wrong, just different, and when we began to accept our differences mentally, we began to experience the joy of mental intimacy.

Thoughts: _____
_____
_____
_____

Action Step: _____
_____

December 9

The following was written by a woman answering our survey.

"Eric never got the best grades in high school when we started dating. I never gave him the credit he deserved, assuming that he didn't measure up. Over the years, I have come to respect his thoughts so much more than I could have imagined.

"My father is someone I have always gone to for advice. I almost always follow his advice. When we were dating and first married, I would find myself arguing with my husband, siding with my father's advice.

"Now that we have focused on being mentally intimate, I want Eric's insights first and foremost. And now there are even many times I don't go to dad for a second opinion. Eric is very intellectually talented. It's just not math and music like me. It's politics, automotive, marketing, and business! I've come to respect him."

Mental intimacy is discovering, identifying, and appreciating the intelligence of your spouse.

Thoughts: _____
_____
_____
_____

Action Step: _____
_____

December 10

Here's a great quote from a woman who wrote us:

"I would honestly say that my spouse is more intelligent than I but over the years I have discovered that although he is a genius, there are areas that he has no clue about such as teaching a classroom of first graders!

"We have become better listeners and have become more acquainted with what each other is interested in and from there our marriage has grown. When you care about someone, you choose to learn about what interests them and then you learn about that topic so that you can have intelligent conversations about it or at least understand what the other is sharing with you as you listen."

Great advice. We cannot expect to become mentally intimate with our spouse without work. we have to discover our spouse's intelligence, choose to learn, listen, and become acquainted with their interests. We have to make a deliberate choice to learn about our spouse, their interests, what makes them tick, and how they are wired.

Thoughts: _____
_____
_____
_____

Action Step: _____
_____

December 11

In this area of mental intimacy, the attractors and detractors could be one and the same.

The biggest detractor to mental intimacy is the misconception that you have to have the same level of education in order to be mentally on the same page. Education is not the issue. The issue is our attitude about intelligence and our willingness to defer to another individual who may understand a concept better than we do.

This is where attitude can be both a detractor and an attractor. If an individual has an attitude of superiority it will be a detractor, but if one understands the fact we all learn differently and has an attitude of deferment, this attitude can be an attractor.

Different learning styles can also be either a detractor or attractor. Jay and I learn differently. Jay learns by doing. I learn by reading and then doing. When working together, we work in our own styles and letting each other learn from their experience. This becomes an attractor.

Thoughts: _____
_____
_____
_____

Action Step: _____
_____

December 12

Over the years I have had the privilege of teaching a number of sales seminars for businesses. Clear communication is essential in sales. One basic fundamental of sales is this: "People buy on emotion and justify with the facts!"

Think about your retirement for an example. Why do you sock money away for retirement? Fear of being without income. Hope of an income in your golden years. Not wanting to be a burden to your children. All good answers and all emotionally based. Even the drive to be a good steward has a significant emotional basis. We buy almost everything on emotion and justify it with the facts.

The same is true in marriage. We "buy" into marriage because of the emotions we are feeling for our spouse. Then we justify staying with that person because of the facts. Maturing and nurturing emotional intimacy in your marriage creates a constant "buy" into the union. The "facts" of our marriage become inconsequential when we realize how emotionally connected we continue to become.

Thoughts: _____
_____
_____

Action Step: _____
_____

December 13

Often when we think of emotion, we think of our souls—the seat of our emotions. We cannot be one without sharing our souls, and quite frankly this is what scares most of us men more than anything else. The idea of sitting with my wife and "sharing" my emotions with her can bring shivers to my spine, and the spines of even the most sensitive men. The "sharing" of emotions is not necessarily emotional intimacy anymore than "sharing" football scores will make your spouse a football fan. Emotional intimacy occurs when you understand and accept your spouse's emotional state. Notice we didn't say you had to like their emotional state, just understand and accept it.

We are all created emotional beings. How we express emotions, however, varies widely. Defining emotional intimacy simply means gaining an understanding of both what makes your spouse feel and then understanding how that emotion plays into daily life. Emotional intimacy breeds forgiveness which is a building block of marriage.

Thoughts: _____
_____
_____
_____

Action Step: _____
_____

December 14

I heard a phrase in college from my dorm mom that I just love. Martha would say, "If you were both the same, one of you wouldn't be necessary." You decide which one (wink, wink).

Seriously, though, if you both had the same emotional make-up, the same mental make-up, the same social make-up, one of you wouldn't be needed.

We can't be the same. Ladies, you don't want your husband to express emotions the same way you do. You married a man, so why complain when he acts like one?

And men, her emotions are real, as real as the adrenalin rush you get when that big buck is in your scope or that fish just took the bait.

In order to build emotional intimacy in your marriage, you must allow your spouse to be the person God created him or her to be, emotions and all!

Thoughts: _____
_____
_____

Action Step: _____
_____

December 15

I want to start by saying that the following is just my opinion. I believe that men feel emotions more intensely than women. I believe when men "feel"--and the truth is they don't "feel" all the time--they do it is on a deep level. Examples? Have you ever seen the joy and exhilaration of a man whose team just won the Super Bowl? Have you ever seen the anger and rage on the face of a man who's lived life on the street? Those are extreme scenarios, but every man identifies with those extreme emotions.

Women attach feeling to everything. They "feel" all the time, and as a result get their feelings hurt easier, enjoy the little things in life more, and generally don't understand how a man can't answer the question, "Honey, how would you feel about chicken for dinner?"

I am not saying one way is right and one is wrong, I simply think a key component to building emotional intimacy is to understand these differences.

Thoughts: _____
_____
_____

Action Step: _____
_____

December 16

We are all emotional beings. As humans, we express emotions different than the next person.

I would even go so far to say that it does not necessarily have to do with whether you are male or female. I think it has more to do with your personality. Jay is the more emotional one in our marriage and I am the more even keeled one. He is more high energy and I more of a stroller through life and those parts of our personalities play into how we express emotions.

I have met a lot of women who do not wear their emotions for the world to see and I have met some men who do! Each of us has a filter that our emotions go through. Some of those filters include loss, guilt, anger, energy, experiences we have lived and the way we see life.

When we get behind our spouses filter and see life from their perspective, we will understand their emotional make up more clearly.

Thoughts: _____
_____
_____
_____

Action Step: _____
_____

December 17

Have you ever wondered what this thing called marriage is all about?

We believe that the purpose of marriage can be found in Mark 10-6-8: Jesus says, "But at the beginning of creation God 'made them male and female. For this reason a man will leave his father and mother and be united to his wife, and the two will become one flesh.' So they are no longer two, but one flesh."

The purpose of marriage is to act as single unit, a team in every aspect of life. For example, when your kids come and ask if they can spend the night at a friends house. Instead of answering right away, just simply reply that you will talk to mom.dad and let them know.

It really lets your kids see you and your spouse working as a team!

Thoughts: _____
_____
_____

Action Step: _____
_____

December 18

Would you rather have a marriage that's efficient or effective? Every team needs a good strategy, and marriage is no different. A good strategy for your marriage is to operate as a team

It isn't always easy to act as a single unit, a team. Let's be honest, sometimes it would be more efficient to do our own thing. Not to wait on your spouse to make a decision, but rather make it quickly and without consultation.

To go ahead and buy that car because you know what the family needs and it just makes sense to buy it now while it is on sale. Or, I know what the kids need for back to school so I am just going to go ahead and by it all because I know what is best, we can talk about budget later.

But is it more effective?

Acting as a team is more effective in the long run and better for the health of your marriage.

Thoughts: _____
_____
_____

Action Step: _____
_____

December 19

Acting as a team in marriage is not as hard or difficult as it sounds. It can be quite simple actually. Here is a great tool you can implement right now and it will impact your marriage.

Change your vocabulary!

Instead of using the words I, me, and mine; uss us, we, and our.

When talking about your kids: "We have great kids."

When talking about your conflicts: "Our problem is…"

I was watching golf on the TV, and noticed that a lot of the younger players use the word "we" when discussing their game. They are seeing themselves and their caddy as a team.

If they can do it in golf, can't we do it in our marriages?

Thoughts: _____
_____
_____
_____

Action Step: _____
_____

December 20

What do you want to leave your kids when you die? Some might answer money....mine will spend it, or fight over it!

I want to leave my kids 4 gifts:

- A love of Jesus--more than anything else to have an intimate relationship with the creator of the universe! I have tried to model a daily walk with Christ and I pray they have seen it.
- A love of others--having compassion for others not only in our back yards or in our daily lives but those less fortunate than us.
- The ability to make good decisions--thinking before acting is always a good motto and not one I have perfected, but hope my kids have caught the value of it.
- A quality work ethic--work is a gift from God. While some say it's our curse, I believe in Christ's Kingdom, a quality work ethic brings glory to God.

Money is not the best thing you can leave your kids. Leave them a legacy that will build their character not their bank account.

Thoughts: _____
_____
_____
_____

Action Step: _____
_____

December 21

Why does my husband seem so angry?

Here a few tips for understanding anger in our men!

1. Understand that while you as a woman feel all the time, men feel more deeply.

2. Don't automatically assume that, just because he is angry, he is angry with you.

3. Anger is not always a bad thing. Having and experiencing this emotion shows that your husband cares about whatever he is angry about.

4. At times there are reasons he is angry, tactful, sincere conversation is necessary here. Most of the time the first question I ask when Jay is angry is is he hungry! WE call it hangry in our house!

Thoughts: _____
_____
_____

Action Step: _____
_____

December 22

Gallant warriors or gentleman?

No we are not talking about the latest Xbox game. We are talking about chivalry!

I am not sure our current culture even understands what it means anymore! I love to see a young man open the car door for his date. I love it when one of our daughter's dates comes to the door to pick her up!

Women, don't settle for something less than a gentleman who will open doors, suffer through a chick flick for you, or even walk on the traffic side of the sidewalk! If your husband doesn't normally do these type of things, let him know how important it is, and teach your sons to learn these habits.

Chivalry is not dead, it is alive and well!

Thoughts: _____
_____
_____
_____

Action Step: _____
_____

December 23

Why does he never listen to me?

It isn't that he isn't listening, we just communicate differently!

I communicate about facts and activities--you know, baseball stats and fishing trips. You communicate about people and feelings--that's why you wants to tell him what everyone said over lunch.

The fact that we communicate differently is why Jay's eyes roll whenever I talk about the person who cut me off in the grocery store, and my eyes roll when he tell me about his golf game.

Ladies here is what I know-if you are talking to him and he has the tv on or is on his tablet or phone--he isn't hearing you!

If you have something to tell him or say to him--make him stop what he's doing and look you in the eyes. Then he hears you!

Thoughts: _____
_____
_____

Action Step: _____
_____

December 24

Chances are you have two very different opinions of what "clean" means.

Laura has this philosophy: if you can't see it, it isn't a mess! My sock drawer for example--I pull it open, socks will explode out of it, and I pick two to wear, they don't have to match. I shove them back in and nobody's the wiser!

Jay, on the other hand, serves a God of order and as a result, I like to have my socks organized by color and kind. All black dress, all black golf socks, all white athletic, all patterned, etc!

When it comes to the house and dishes, vaccuming, dusting, etc. we have asked what is fair. What is fair to each of us and our expectations.

We're both busy, we have kids...what is fair. Make a plan and live by it!

Thoughts: _____
_____
_____
_____

Action Step: _____
_____

December 25

Is an argument always a bad thing? Disagreements can actually be healthy for a marriage, or any relationship! I read once that the number one indicator of divorce isn't hate or lack of love, or even fighting! It's the habitual avoidance of conflict. You are two different people with two different perspectives. You are going to disagree!

We are talking about having a healthy debate about what each other thinks or feels. Another word could be arguing. Respecting each other thoughts and feelings, but still standing by your own opinion, shows you care enough about your marriage or relationship to agree to disagree. That is what makes a marriage healthy and lasting.

A couple who can argue respectfully is a couple that cares about their relationship!

Thoughts: _____
_____
_____

Action Step: _____
_____

December 26

We don't realise it when we get married, but a time comes when it is just the two of you!

For some of us it is our entire marriage--we never had kids.

For others, our marriage has been about the kids! Now they are gone!

First problem here- marriage should never be about the kids! We have kids, and we love our kids! We have great memories, and many more to make. However, all too often people neglect their marriage relationship for our kids.

We need to continue to date each other, develop hobbies we can do as a couple, nurture that friendship over the years! When we do this, we show our kids what a healthy marriage looks like!

Thoughts: _____
_____
_____
_____

Action Step: _____
_____

December 27

I said I do now, I can say I don't.

It sometimes seems that we stand at the altar and treat it like a finish line. We got we wanted--our spouse--so now we can relax, we have completed the race to marriage.

I don't have to shop with you. I don't have to watch football with you. We don't even have to talk.

Oh, but wait--yes you do! When we adopt this finish line attitude, we begin to take each other and the marriage for granted. We must keep the spark alive each and every day.

One very simple, but not easy, way to do that is with 5-10 minutes of uninterrupted conversation every day with your spouse. Over coffee, over lunch, after dinner, after kids are in bed...whenever you do it, just do it.

So, pour a cup of coffee and begin!

Thoughts: _____
_____
_____
_____

Action Step: _____
_____

December 28

We all have those things that make our skin crawl or teeth tingle. Those pet peeves that can send us over the edge. Unfortunately, our spouse probably possesses a few of those that can really get our goat!

For me, I can't stand it when I am talking to Jay and he interrupts me with a thought he has that has nothing to do with what I was saying.

Here is the deal though, if I focused on that all the time, I would be an unhappy, bitter woman. Instead, what we need to do is wake up everyday looking for something positive today in our spouse. Hit the reset button, so to speak, everyday.

Thoughts: _____
_____
_____

Action Step: _____
_____

December 29

So, I am a big scaredy cat when it comes to thunder storms! I had to lay in a ditch at girl scout camp as a 10 year-old during a tornado, and just have not liked storms since.

The other night we had a doozie of a storm. I was nervous and antsy. I kept watching out the window at the howling winds and blowing rain. Finally, Jay asked, "do you want to go in the basement?"

That's love, folks! He knew instinctively that I was uncomfortable but felt silly all at the same time! He made the suggestion out of respect for my fear.

Grace, Jay, and I sat in the basement for about 10 minutes, and no one ever laughed at me for my over reaction to the storm.

How can you instinctively help your spouse today?

Thoughts: _____
_____
_____

Action Step: _____
_____

December 30

Every week, sometimes more than once, we go to the grocery together. It is just what we do. Sometimes we have other errands to run or we do lunch beforehand out, but it is like our weekly date to get groceries.

What is your weekly date? Maybe it is watching your favorite TV show together. Or maybe you get a cup of coffee together. We have friends that walk together every morning.

Whatever it might be, keep doing it! If you don't have something you do together, as a date or activity. find one! Fit it in your schedule. Make it happen. Your marriage will be better because of it!

Thoughts: _____
_____
_____
_____

Action Step: _____
_____

December 31

I used to be a screamer! I screamed at my husband, I screamed at my kids, I screamed at the really bad driver that cut me off!

At first Jay thought, "maybe she's just having a bad day." Then when multiple days strung together, he knew this was just part of the package...

But I have changed. It started with my kids. I got really tired of seeing them frightened whenever I would raise my voice. So I decided to do something different.

Whenever my kids annoyed me, sassed me, or spilt milk, I counted to 10 before I said anything. It worked with them so I began doing it when Jay annoyed me....

I am no longer a screamer!

Thoughts: _____
_____
_____

Action Step: _____
_____

Made in the USA
Columbia, SC
26 November 2017